Marxist Left Review is a peer-reviewed theoretical journal published twice-yearly by Socialist Alternative, a revolutionary organisation based in Australia.

We aim to engage with theoretical and political debates on the Australian and international left, making a rigorous yet accessible case for Marxist politics. We also seek to provide analysis of the social, political and economic dynamics shaping Australian capitalism.

Unless indicated otherwise all articles published reflect the views of the individual author.

We need our readers' support to continue publication.

Subscribe at marxistleftreview.org

Marxist Left Review

For day-to-day news and analysis, Socialist Alternative also publishes a fortnightly newspaper, *Red Flag*.

Read online and subscribe at redflag.org.au

REDFLAG

NEW BOOKS NOW AVAILABLE

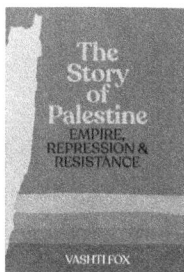

Vashti Fox
**The Story of Palestine:
Empire, Repression & Resistance**

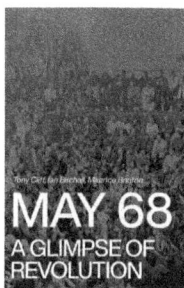

T Cliff, I Birchall
**May 68 –
A Glimpse of
Revolution**

A Lunacharsky
**Revolutionary
Silhouettes**

R Leviné-Meyer
**Leviné:
The Life of a
Revolutionary**

John Molyneux
**Anarchism:
A Marxist
Critique**

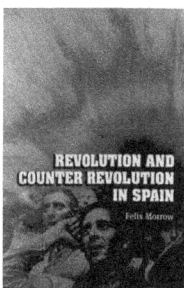

Felix Morrow
**Revolution
and Counter
Revolution
in Spain**

F Raskolnikov
**Kronstadt
and Petrograd
in 1917**

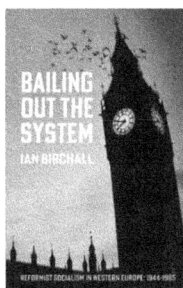

Ian Birchall
**Bailing out
the System**

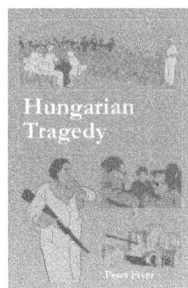

Peter Fryer
**Hungarian
Tragedy**

mlr

Marxist Left Review

Number 20 – Winter 2020

Editor
Omar Hassan

Editorial Committee
Mick Armstrong
Sandra Bloodworth
Omar Hassan
Louise O'Shea

Reviews Editor
Alexis Vassiley

© Social Research Institute

Published by Socialist Alternative
Melbourne, July 2020

PO Box 4354
Melbourne University, VIC 3052

www.marxistleftreview.org
marxistleftreview@gmail.com

Contributions to *Marxist Left Review* are peer-reviewed

ISSN 1838-2932
rrp. $17

Subediting and proofreading
Tess Lee Ack
Diane Fieldes
Sagar Sanyal
Sam Pietsch

Layout and production
Oscar Sterner

Cover
James Plested

Printed by IngramSpark

CONTENTS

MICK ARMSTRONG

The NSW BLF: The battle to tame the concrete jungle[1]

Mick Armstrong has been actively involved in socialist politics since the late 1960s. He is the author of numerous pamphlets and articles on revolutionary organisation and the Australian labour movement, including *The Industrial Workers of the World in Australia* and *The Labor Party: A Marxist analysis.*

IN A SERIES of spectacular industrial battles the NSW Builders Labourers' Federation (BLF) dramatically improved the wages and working conditions of a group of workers who had long been at the very bottom of the pile in the construction industry. Workers who had previously been too embarrassed to admit what job they did now proudly proclaimed themselves BLs. This growing self-confidence and assertiveness led them to directly confront the bosses for control over the construction industry. The BLs demanded that they have a decisive say over what was built or not built in the interests of the working class as a whole and the mass of the oppressed. This was most famously expressed in the form of the Green Bans which shut down a massive array of environmentally destructive projects. The BLF's flamboyant leader, the recently deceased Jack Mundey, became far and away Australia's most notorious Communist.

At its high point in the early 1970s the NSW BLF was easily the most radical union – in terms of industrial militancy, democratic rank and file control and determined action around a broad sweep of political causes – in the post-war period in Australia. You would have to go right back to the Marxist and

---

1. This article is dedicated to the memory of my comrade Dave Shaw – a BLF militant and revolutionary socialist – who gave his life in the battle to tame the concrete jungle. The title is inspired by Pete Thomas's 1973 booklet.

revolutionary syndicalist-led Amalgamated Miners' Association (AMA) in Broken Hill during the First World War, or even earlier to the syndicalist Sydney Rockchoppers Union, to see a comparable union.[2]

The BLs' path-breaking role was not just confined to Green Bans. With their militant democratic approach they forthrightly challenged the entrenched bureaucratic apparatuses that dominated the union movement, both left and right. They campaigned with concerted industrial action around all the political issues confronting working-class people and the oppressed – racism, the Vietnam War, poverty, women's rights, health services, decent housing, adequate pensions and public services. They sought to act as the tribune of the people.

This class struggle approach made them an incredible array of enemies – most obviously the building bosses, the capitalist media, the cops and governments of all political hues. However their most insidious enemies proved to be the bureaucrats who ran the rest of the union movement. Indeed the agent of their destruction was Norm Gallagher, the supposedly left-wing Maoist Federal BLF Secretary, funded by and acting at the behest of the building bosses. Gallagher's thuggery was cheered on by the head of the ACTU, Bob Hawke. Meanwhile the other main left union in the industry, the Building Workers Industrial Union (BWIU), led by the pro-Moscow Socialist Party of Australia, sat on its hands, happy to see its militant rival obliterated. Key unions led by Mundey's fellow Communist Party of Australia (CPA) members also refused to come to the aid of the NSW BLF, as they too looked askance at its strident radicalism and commitment to rank and file union democracy.

As a result, NSW BLF was eventually defeated, crushed by superior forces. But it left a shining example of what working-class people are capable of. It is an example, with both enormous strengths and some significant weaknesses, which

---

2. For the AMA see Kennedy 1978 and Adams 2010. For the Rockchoppers' Union see Sheldon 1988.

deserves to be studied in detail by socialists today as they fight for a revolutionary, class struggle orientation in the union movement.

Long dedicated work[3]

This radical union had its origins in a tiny rank and file group established by a handful of CPA members in 1951. The NSW BLF was at that point a right-wing, gangster-run affair in the pocket of the bosses. One prominent militant, Ralph Kelly, maintains that BLF organisers picked up a five pound note from the boss on each job they visited and never worried about the safety conditions "or anything else".[4]

Workers who made a stand were bashed on the job or at union meetings by thugs at times armed with revolvers, or sacked after been fingered as a "trouble maker" by an official. After World War II Communists had been expelled from the BLF, and for a period in the 1950s they were barred from holding official positions. The hallmark of a militant in these years was a list of repeated sackings. Jack Mundey only survived in the industry in the 1950s by working on small suburban jobs which BLF organisers rarely visited. "One year I had as many as seventeen jobs; as soon as I started work one of the organisers would arrive and point me out to the boss."[5]

Builders' labourers were the lowest of the low in the construction industry; subject to poor pay, punishing, unsafe work and treated with utter contempt by their employers. Accidents and deaths on the job were rife. Amenities, such as eating sheds and toilets, were worse than non-existent. They often had to provide their own pick and shovel. As one militant Keith Jessop stated:

> The industry was in a very bad way... There was little or no

---

3. The most detailed accounts of the development of the Rank and File Committee are Burgmann 1981 and True 1995.
4. Burgmann 1981, pvii.
5. True 1995, p37.

mechanisation... Brickies and plasterers were looked after by hod carriers and all the steel reinforcement was bent on the site, which was extremely hard work. There was no payment for public holidays; there was no wet weather pay, no annual leave and no sick leave. In all, it was a very hard, arduous, dusty and dirty and thankless job.[6]

It took long years of dedicated work by a determined group of rank and file Communists to start turning that around. After 18 months of activity they held their first open meeting, which attracted 15 workers, five of whom were CPers. They began to produce a roneoed newssheet, *Hoist*, dealing with job issues initially every two or three months. As they became more established, *Hoist* went monthly.

They received organisational support from the CPA and some assistance from the Communist-led BWIU, which covered carpenters and bricklayers. However as Joe Ferguson, one of the founders of the Rank and File Committee, explained:

> The main thing was to get the *Hoist* round the jobs. Also we used to go and see a lot of blokes on the weekend. The BWIU used to give us the names of delegates who weren't bad blokes, and we used to go round and see them...have a yarn with them. We built up the organisation that way. It was just a lot of patient work.[7]

Hoist played a vital organisational role. They cohered a network of supporters by raising money for it on the job via the likes of raffles, and establishing a machine to distribute it. Through this work they gradually established a broader rank and file movement that, though largely led by CPers, included left-wing ALP members and other militants. They sought to build shop steward organisation on the job to give workers the confidence to fight back. In 1956 a huge construction project – a munitions

6.   Mallory 2005, pp94-95.
7.   True 1995, pp16-17.

complex – started at St Marys in Western Sydney, employing 4,000 workers. Joe Ferguson stated:

> There was a thousand builders labourers on it. There would have been about 20 builders labourers delegates on the job, we had about 15 of them supporting the Rank and File.[8]

Jack Mundey joined the BLF in March 1957 and became chair of the shop stewards' committee at the Clyde Oil Refinery. Mundey had previously joined the CPA in 1955:

> I joined the Communist Party as a militant worker who judged communists...as the most consistent fighters for better wages and working conditions on the factory floor and as people who wanted to make life better for ordinary workers. The communists put forward positive ideas about a more even distribution of wealth of the country and that suited my egalitarian ideas.[9]

Another prominent militant Tom Hogan added:

> The thing that made me join the CP...was the fact of the hard work... the hours that fellows were prepared to put into it. They were giving the real leadership on those jobs...the people I had been warned against were the people I felt closest to – Jack, Bert McGill, Joe Ferguson, Kevin Gledhill and Harry Connell.[10]

According to Mundey, when he joined the Rank and File Committee: "The intellectual person in the builders labourers in my opinion was Joe Ferguson, the best orator was Harry Connell who was the secretary of the Rank and File, and it consisted of about 8 or 10 people at that stage."[11]

Ferguson and Connell were both Communists and the role of the politically trained Communist militants was vital. Many of the new activists were politically unformed. As long-term

---

8. True 1995, p22.
9. Mundey 1981, p23.
10. Burgmann 1981, pix.
11. True 1995, p24.

militant Darcy Duggan put it, "they had union consciousness but no political consciousness...the only thing they had in common was a tendency to get sacked".[12] As the Rank and File Committee's influence grew they were able to mobilise more union members to branch meetings. They were in Jack Mundey's words "sincere, not necessarily militant, workers opposed to the corrupt Thomas leadership".[13]

Things began to change with the building boom of the 1950s and 1960s. A plethora of inner city high rise construction projects led to a rapidly expanding workforce with greater skills on larger sites, and consequently greater potential industrial power for labourers. As buildings became higher the accident rate soared and safety became a fundamental issue. Militants began to establish a strong camaraderie and organise together after work in the pubs around Sydney's Circular Quay, where a number of key projects, such as the Opera House, the AMP building, British Tobacco, Goldfields and the huge State Office Block, were concentrated.

From 1957 onwards hundreds of BLs attended union branch meetings and the Rank and File began to control them. On that basis they had high hopes for the three-yearly union elections in 1958 – the first they contested. But the elections were thoroughly rigged by the right-wing machine. In the aftermath there was significant demoralisation and a group of about 500 riggers and scaffolders – the more militant and more skilled section of the labourers – broke away to form their own union. This significant minority of the member-ship were fed up with the BLF and were hostile to both the Australian Workers Union (AWU) and the Ironworkers Union (FIA), the other right-wing unions that covered them on some jobs. The breakaway survived for a couple of years before fading away.

Nonetheless the Rank and File managed to weather the

---

12. Burgmann 1981, pvii.
13. Burgmann 1981, piv.

storm and further build support. As Joe Ferguson put it: "Basically we built up a network... It came to a position where we started to run the jobs with the workers on the job, not the union".[14] Activists like Jack Mundey and Bert McGill were paid from collections on the job "for weeks at a time to go round Newcastle, Wollongong and city jobs, delivering *Hoist*, getting to know workers and getting them along to meetings... We controlled every monthly meeting in that period".[15]

They managed to have McGill and Mick McNamara, a young raw "cleanskin", elected as temporary organisers at a branch meeting. When the executive moved McNamara out of the city to isolate him, "eight or nine big jobs stopped and marched to the office".[16] They caught the officials in the pub and forced them to back down.

The corrupt right-wing leadership was defeated in the 1961 elections by a coalition of the Rank and File Committee and more moderate forces. The Rank and File did a deal with some centre ALPers not to contest a few positions. The majority of the Rank and File backed the inexperienced ALP left-winger McNamara for state secretary in order to get the pro-Labor vote. A few militants, who were later to back the Maoist Communist Party of Australia (Marxist Leninist), argued to back Jack Mundey for Secretary. Mundey himself subsequently claimed that it would have been "adventurist" for him, as a known communist, to take the secretary position at that time.[17] So essentially they ran a "Broad Left" team that won 17 out of 21 positions.

Mundey failed to win an organiser's position in 1961. "It was an anti-communist vote."[18] But Mundey, who was playing an increasingly central role, was elected temporary city organiser in 1962 and state secretary in 1968.

14. True 1995, p39.
15. Burgmann 1981, pv.
16. Burgmann 1981, pxi.
17. Burgmann 1981, pxiv.
18. Burgmann 1981, pxvi.

The new leadership was virtually starting from scratch and spent a great deal of effort in its first few years essentially creating a union out of the disastrous wreck that the old corrupt leadership had left behind. It was deep in debt, had no proper administrative apparatus, and the old right had even burnt the minutes books to cover their crimes.

The new leadership built up a network of job delegates from 29 at the end of 1961 to over 130 by December 1963. They went on to comfortably win elections in 1964 and again in 1967. Industrially they initially took a reasonably cautious approach. They did not defy court orders or the anti-union Penal Powers, something they would do in later years. They were strongly supportive of the ALP and of then ALP leader Arthur Calwell. In February 1964 Mundey moved that the union "call upon the entire membership to mount the best possible campaign to help defeat the Menzies Government, and elect a Federal Labor Government".[19] A delicate balance was maintained on the executive between CPers and ALP members. However there were not major ideological differences, reflected in the fact that ALPer Mick McNamara visited Russia in 1967, as did Mundey in 1969, and a number of the ALP activists were later to join the CPA.

The main difference with other left unions was that the new leadership adopted a much more democratic approach. As Mundey explained: "Because of the way in which the crime element [had] controlled our union it meant that we had to develop a highly democratic alternative".[20] Lively branch meetings decided union policy. Job delegate conferences were established and began to play an important role in directing activities. In order to keep close to the rank and file, BLF organisers rejected a move to increase their own wages.

One important overhead of having the new leadership in office was that the Rank and File Committee became less active,

19. Burgmann 1981, pxxvi.
20. Burgmann 1981, pxxxiii.

with meetings held irregularly. Workers instead looked to the democratic structures of the union and to the new officials to do the job for them. This is a recurring problem and underlines the importance of building strong, workplace-based organisation to help maintain rank and file involvement and day-to-day democratic control.

Hoist tended to be more commonly produced in election years. And after the 1964 elections when the Rank and File team won complete control, the Rank and File Committee was put into abeyance. Its main function in subsequent years was the pre-selection of election candidates, though it did continue to play a social role with large fundraising BBQs attracting up to 500 members.

Mundey described the leadership elected in 1964 as "still orthodox militant but further to the left than we'd been before".[21] It mainly fought around basic bread and butter issues of wages and conditions on the job, but as it became more assertive this laid the basis for a more radical stand. The leadership also took up political issues such as Aboriginal rights and nuclear disarmament, but at this stage its approach was not markedly different from that of other left-wing unions of the period, such as the Waterside Workers, the Miners or the Seamen. The BLs did not, as they were to do later, take industrial action around political issues.

Not long after the 1967 elections, in which the Rank and File team was re-elected unopposed, Mick McNamara stood down as secretary and Mundey was appointed temporarily in his place and then convincingly won a rank and file ballot. His acceptance speech concentrated on improved administrative, organisational and financial issues. As Meredith Burgmann comments: "There is little in the above to forecast the radical changes that were to take place".[22]

By the late sixties the mood across the working class was

21. Burgmann 1981, pxlvi.
22. Burgmann 1981, pl.

shifting dramatically.[23] There was a surge in strike action, particularly in the metal trades, with many localised strikes outside the framework of the arbitration system. Shop steward organisation strengthened markedly. The upsurge came to a head in the "Absorption" battle of 1968 when shop committees in the metal trades co-ordinated a wave of strikes which smashed employers' attempts to absorb a wage increase granted by the Arbitration Commission. The "Absorption" victory fuelled confidence to take on the hated Penal Powers – the anti-union laws of the day – that were increasingly being used to fine unions for strike action. The crunch came in May 1969 with the jailing of Tramways union secretary Clarrie O'Shea.[24] Concerted nationwide strikes forced O'Shea's release and turned the Penal Powers into a dead letter. The floodgates opened for a prolonged working-class offensive that won massive gains.

The upsurge in strikes and working-class confidence intersected with and reinforced a growing society-wide political radicalisation, sparked at first by young people on university campuses, notably around opposition to the Vietnam War. The NSW BLF was to be swept up in and transformed by these developments, becoming one of its most radical components.

The Communist Party and the BLF

Communist Party Secretary Laurie Aarons maintains that the CPA's struggle against the corrupt BLF leadership had been "more or less continuous" from the forties onwards and that "it was the Party and virtually only the Party involved".[25] These claims seem accurate. Moreover, while the Rank and File-backed leadership elected in 1961 contained a significant ALP component, by 1969 CPers dominated the leadership. Consequently it is impossible to understand developments in

---

23. For this period see Bramble 2008.
24. For the Clarrie O'Shea strike see Wood 2013.
25. Burgmann 1981, piii.

the BLF without an overview of the CPA's political approach, particularly its trade union strategy. The CPA also had long had a strong ideological influence on the ALP left, which was commonly Stalinist in the post-war years.

In its pre-Stalinist years in the 1920s the CPA, after the split from the party of the Trades Hall Reds – a group of left officials around NSW Labor Council Secretary Jock Garden – began to develop a rank and file strategy based on the experience of the Minority Movement in Britain.[26] This revolutionary strategy sought to organise rank and file workers independently of the union bureaucracy and to pursue the class struggle aggressively when the officials would not lead.

This approach emphasised the importance of building strong shop steward organisation, shop committees uniting rank and file delegates of all the unions on the job, area committees of shop stewards and union-wide rank and file committees based on a militant class struggle policy. The rank and file strategy was predicated on a Marxist analysis that saw the union bureaucracy as an inherently conservative social layer that was loyal to capitalism. The union bureaucracy's social interests were seen as counterposed to those of the mass of the working class, and it would need to be taken on and defeated if workers were to overthrow capitalism. This revolutionary approach was and still is sharply counterposed to the standard left-reformist orientation of establishing electoral coalitions or reform groups to capture the leadership of unions and change them from the top down.

The ability of the early CP to build a Minority Movement was limited by a series of factors: the party's small size (only a few hundred members in the mid-1920s), continuing theoretical confusion on the question and the fact that the Communist International in Russia opportunistically sought to maintain an alliance with Garden's Trades Hall Reds and vetoed attempts

---

26. For the Minority Movement see Cliff and Gluckstein 1986, Martin 1969 and Woodhouse and Pearce 1975.

to form Minority Movement groups in Labor Council affiliates. This essentially limited the CPA to a Minority Movement group in the powerful miners' union, which was not a Labor Council affiliate.[27]

All this abruptly changed in the early 1930s with the Stalinisation of the CPA and the enforcement on Moscow's orders of the sectarian Third Period policy. Union officials of all stripes were now denounced as social-fascists – more dangerous than the actual fascists – and an aggressive attempt was made to form Minority Movement groups across the board. Given the utter bankruptcy of the union bureaucracy's response to the employers' onslaught in the Great Depression, the Minority Movement's denunciation of officials and strident militancy struck a chord in militant sections, such as the coal miners who had been deeply embittered after a 15-month lockout. So despite the absurd rhetorical flourishes and substantial tactical errors flowing from the international line, the CP managed to grow to a few thousand members by the mid-1930s.

This all changed when Moscow imposed the class-collaborationist Popular Front strategy in the mid-1930s. Suddenly the CPA's approach to union work shifted markedly to the right and became increasingly bureaucratic. This bureaucratic degeneration was compounded by the CPA's success in winning more and more official positions. Rank and file opposition groups were still encouraged in right-wing-controlled unions but soon fell into abeyance once Communists or their supporters won control. Union officials came to dominate CPA union work, and rank and file Communists, let alone the mass of workers, had little democratic control over them.

In notorious cases like the Ironworkers' union, Communists built hard line bureaucratic machines that bashed and purged left-wing dissidents. In unions with stronger democratic traditions, such as the Amalgamated Engineering Union, where Communists shared power with other forces, the

---

27. See Armstrong 2013 for this period.

CPA's approach to industrial questions often differed little from that of ALP officials.

During World War II the CPA adopted an ultra-patriotic pro-war line and stridently opposed strikes, going as far as organising strike breakers. After the war, in the context of a huge working-class upsurge, the party gradually moved left, a trend that accelerated as the Cold War heated up in the late 1940s. But it was a top down, bureaucratic militancy which undermined the party's capacity to successfully lead struggles and contributed to the disastrous defeat of the 1949 coal strike.

In the early 1950s, under the conservatising pressures of Cold War isolation and Russia's new line, the CPA moved to a more right-wing stance. As historian Ian Turner notes, the right-wing Grouper-led unions "concerned to establish their industrial legitimacy, were now just as likely to be involved in more limited industrial actions as were the communist-led unions".[28] In union elections the CPA pursued a policy of "unity tickets" with ALP members on a lowest common denominator basis.

As late as 1965 CPA leader Laurie Aarons stated that communists wanted cooperation with both the right and left of the ALP and that the CPA did not want to dominate the unions.[29] Aarons had a track record as a hard-line Stalinist, who had very much led the charge against anti-Stalinist dissidents in the aftermath of the 1956 Russian invasion of Hungary and wrote a ferocious defence of the traditional Stalinist line in a pamphlet called *Party of the Working Class*.[30] Yet installed as new CPA secretary, he began to edge the party, at first tentatively, in a more liberal direction.

Initially the move away from hard-core Stalinism did not represent a shift to the left. However a radical wave was beginning to emerge in Australia and internationally that was

28. Turner 1978, pp112-113.
29. Davidson 1969, pp156-159.
30. O'Lincoln 1985, p108.

considerably less enthused by the bureaucratic Russian model of supposed socialism. As this radicalisation deepened in 1968 and 1969, new political forces emerged, particularly on campus, which began to challenge the CPA's overwhelming dominance of the left. The Aarons leadership, fearful that the CPA's dull, conservative, bureaucratic practice meant that it was missing the bus, began to shift further left in an attempt to co-opt the young radicals. In January 1969 the CPA national committee urged a "bolder confrontation with the penal powers".[31]

The edging away from Stalinism and the adoption of a more radical approach was strongly resisted by entrenched forces in the party, in particular established union bureaucrats such as the BWIU's Pat Clancy. As early as the 1967 CPA Congress Clancy had crossed swords with Aarons and defended a parliamentary-oriented reformist policy and a top-down bureaucratic approach in the unions. In the lead up to the 1970 CPA Congress the divisions became increasingly open, with Aarons arguing:

> A key issue will remain that between the two differing concepts of unionism: either a democratic movement based upon active participation of its members in workshop or organisation, its methods always based upon mass action, or a movement run from the top, committed to arbitration and legalism and thus absorbed into the system.[32]

Aarons deplored CPA union officials' hostility to criticism: "When youth are solemnly warned not to criticise union officials lest this be destructive, then revolutionary spirit has been lost".[33] This opened up more space for genuine militants in the party, such as those in the NSW BLF, to have their heads.

But though shifting left, the approach of the Aarons leadership was far from being Marxist. It was a liberal humanist approach that did not see the working class as *the* decisive force

---

31. Bramble 2008, p45.
32. Mallory 2005, p84.
33. O'Lincoln 1985, p145.

in the struggle for socialism. The CPA still viewed Russia and Eastern Europe as a form of socialism. The Stalinist states just needed liberal democracy tacked onto them. Consequently the Aarons leadership enthusiastically supported Dubček's liberal reforming Stalinist regime in Czechoslovakia that was overthrown by Russian tanks in August 1968. The Russian invasion, according to BLF leader Joe Owens, hit the Sydney building industry "like a time bomb".[34] There were physical clashes on building sites between hard-line pro-Russian Stalinists and supporters of the CPA's criticism of the Russian invasion.

Leading BLF CPA members such as Jack Mundey, Harry Hatfield and Tom and Brian Hogan played a prominent role in the fight against the conservative forces around Pat Clancy. Clancy resigned from the CPA in October 1971 and became chairman of the pro-Moscow Socialist Party of Australia (SPA) on its foundation in December 1971. He accused the CPA of being overtaken by "ultra radicals" and of failing to form an alliance with the ALP.[35] The SPA repeatedly denounced supposed "Trotskyite" influence in the party.

The CPA's jag to the left deepened with the massive upsurge of struggle at the beginning of the seventies. Ever since the Popular Front days of the 1930s the CPA had argued for a nationalist alliance with supposedly progressive Australian capitalists against "foreign" capitalists. Now, reflecting the more left-wing mood, the CPA began to downplay nationalism, just as Maoists such as Norm Gallagher embraced increasingly reactionary nationalist politics. In 1973 Aarons attacked as a "retreat" the Maoists' "old concept of the 'national bourgeoisie' with whom workers can supposedly unite against foreign capital".[36]

In the early 1970s the CPA talked a lot about workers'

---

34. Burgmann 1981, p338.
35. Mallory 2005, p90.
36. O'Lincoln 1985, p163.

control and a "new concept of unionism". Though generally pretty vague and woolly, this rhetoric significantly impacted the BLF, who seriously tried to put the idea of workers' control into effect. It did so much more seriously than any other union the CPA influenced. This reflected the changing nature of the construction industry, the history of the BLF militants and the fact that the prominent CPers had taken over the leadership of the union at a time of soaring militancy. They had not settled into becoming entrenched bureaucrats. The BLF became the symbol of the CPA's more radical, less Stalinist face. The increasingly militant stance of the NSW BLF led many of the best activists to join the CPA. Something like 100 BLs became party members.

The main political document for the 1974 CPA Congress described the party as "an independent revolutionary party working for socialist revolution". Indeed the document used the word "revolution" or "revolutionary" 54 times in nine pages. "Yet", as Tom O'Lincoln writes, "within a few years all the radical rhetoric was being disavowed, and the party was on its way to a new right wing consensus".[37]

In 1970 CPA activist Joyce Slater had written in a letter to the party paper *Tribune*:

> The extreme Rightwing Stalinists have taken a beating, but what of the stay-putters, don't rock-the-boat elements in the middle? We have only just begun the fight for radical change in the party.[38]

The reality was that fight was never pursued to a conclusion. The shift to the left was thinly based. Although the NSW CPA used the radical prestige of the BLF to recruit young activists, and Jack Mundey was installed as CPA president, the party did not fundamentally change. It was in no sense a revolutionary organisation. By the mid-seventies the CPA leaders were moving relentlessly in an explicitly reformist direction, becoming key

---

37. O'Lincoln 1985, pp145-146.
38. O'Lincoln 1985, p153.

architects of the wage-cutting Prices and Incomes Accord of the 1980s.

The CPA in the 1970s became a loose amalgam of disparate forces. An entrenched right wing dominant in Victoria did little to sell *Tribune* which it considered too radical. It was not just the likes of Pat Clancy, who had left to join the SPA, who decried the BLF's "adventurism". Many CPA union bureaucrats felt threatened by the BLF's militancy and championing of rank and file democracy.

So while the BLF sharply radicalised, the powerful Metal-workers Union, easily the most important union at the time with 180,000 members, in which leading Communists such as Laurie Carmichael and John Halfpenny were prominent, hardly altered course. When Gallagher intervened in 1974 to crush the NSW BLF, the Metalworkers, which had members in important sections of the construction industry, did not lift a finger to support them.

The BLF in its heroic period

A series of militant strikes by BLs in the early 1970s won path-breaking wage increases and much improved conditions. The BLF used a whole range of militant tactics – crane occupations, the breaking or interrupting of concrete pours, flying pickets and the use of organised vigilante squads – to physically destroy work done by scab labour.

The lengthy 1970 "Margins strike", which won very important wage gains, was a key turning point. The strike was democratically controlled by an elected strike committee which included significant migrant representation. The strike committee adopted a new tactic of organised vigilante groups of strikers who visited work sites where scabbing was taking place. In most cases that simply involved talking to workers and convincing them to join the strike. There were, however, some confrontations with bosses, security guards and the cops. A few work sites were occupied by the vigilantes. More controversial, and widely denounced in the media, was the vigilante squads' destruction of work done by scabs. This was a tactic that the NSW BLF became famous for.

After five weeks on strike they had a slashing victory that significantly reduced the pay differential between BLs and carpenters and other trades. This dramatically raised the confidence of the workers involved, as labourers expressed their pride in being part of the union, a BL. A 16-day strike in 1971 won further decisive gains. The NSW BLF managed to keep winning very substantial pay rises right up until the time of Gallagher's federal intervention in October 1974, which brought the victories to an end.

But it was not just these major industry-wide struggles that won improvements. Militancy exploded at the local job level as worker confidence soared. Almost daily battles occurred on individual workplaces to win site allowances and over-award payments. Some jobs, such as Dillingham Constructions' huge Qantas site in Clarence Street, became legendary for militancy under the leadership of a team of experienced activists. An almost four-month-long strike on the Qantas site in 1970 won a substantial site allowance.

Numerous bold, irreverent but effective tactics were tried. On one site, where management failed to provide anything like adequate amenity facilities, workers dumped the pathetic shed they had been given into a deep excavation. They soon got what they were demanding. Breaking concrete pours became a favoured tactic. Dave Shaw recounted:

> You wait till they are about to pour concrete, then you tell the boss you may be holding a meeting, so they stop. They stop the pour, and of course you don't hold a meeting. You do this every day. Once we had the company pouring a yard of concrete in three weeks. They paid $200,000 in wages and got $180 in progress payments.

A very defiant attitude emerged. Workers were no longer intimidated by company managers or the bosses' standover merchants. On some jobs they struck over "the general attitude of the company". Foremen were specifically targeted. Dave Shaw described how "we trapped the general foreman in a large cardboard box, then stacked more boxes around it and on top, up to the ceiling. He was caught for two hours, screaming and shouting".[39]

The BLF went on to win every major battle with the bosses from the 1970 strike until Gallagher's federal intervention. The rising militancy, the path-breaking wage gains and the boom in the construction industry fuelled a major increase in union membership to a peak of about 11,000 in 1973-4. The union leadership was also radicalising. In 1970 Mundey criticised the approach of mainstream union officialdom: "There was too much readiness to *settle* rather than to set out to *win* disputes". He explicitly criticised left-wing officials:

> Most militant workers have been critical for years of the general passivity displayed in strikes, and the failure of communists and others on the left to really force the issues... These workers found it difficult to differentiate who was who, who was left, right or centre when all urged return to work when it came to the prospect of a longer strike.[40]

From 1971 the BLF increasingly pursued an approach that seriously encroached on managerial prerogatives, including resistance to sackings, a form of de-facto union hire and work-ins. In most cases in Australia and internationally, work-ins were employed as a defensive tactic to fight job losses, whereas the BLF repeatedly used work-ins as an aggressive strategy to challenge management's right to hire and fire at will and gain greater control over the workplace, including the election of foremen and safety officers and control over the allocation of specific jobs.

---

39. Shaw 1976, p9.
40. Burgmann and Burgmann 1999, p51.

A key factor underpinning radicalism was the highly democratic nature of the union. Key policies were not imposed by officials but were thoroughly debated out and decided at mass members' meetings. The BLF militants took measures to limit the development of an entrenched union bureaucracy. Organisers regularly returned to work on the job for prolonged periods, and Mundey himself stood down as secretary.

It was the heightened confidence BLs gained from their industrial victories, combined with the political arguments made by socialists in the union, that led builders' labourers to play a prominent role in fighting around a series of political issues – Aboriginal rights, the Vietnam War, opposition to apartheid in South Africa, women's liberation (they championed getting women jobs in a previously all-male industry) and gay rights. Mundey argued that "for a union to be meaningful it must speak up on all issues affecting the life of not only the members of a union but all Australian people".[41]

The BLF did not just endorse left-wing causes in words. It backed them up with serious action and gave us a glimpse of how a broader movement of militant workers could seriously challenge capitalist exploitation and defend the rights of the oppressed. When draft resisters sought refuge at the Sydney University Student Union, BLs built barricades to keep the police out. In 1971 the BLF strongly backed protests against apartheid in South Africa when the all-white South African rugby league team toured Australia. Jack Mundey declared:

> We think it is not good enough to just demonstrate and protest. We feel at least some of the games must be physically stopped. We consider we will go down in the eyes of the world as a racist country unless some of the games are stopped.

NSW BLF President Bob Pringle and another worker were arrested for sawing through the goal posts at the Sydney Cricket

41. Burgmann and Burgmann 1999, p52.

Ground. And Mundey was charged with contempt of court after declaring that "the two men would have been jailed if we hadn't demonstrated and considered a national strike".[42]

In 1972-73 the BLF waged a long campaign against property developers in Redfern to secure low-cost housing for the local Aboriginal community. In July 1972 Mundey was arrested in the course of campaigning against the Vietnam War on a charge of "intent to incite" people not to register for National Service. In the middle of 1973 the BLF banned construction work at Macquarie University in protest at the expulsion of Jeremy Fisher from a residential college because he was gay. The authorities were forced to reinstate him. This was a path-breaking action for gay rights in a period when homophobia was still incredibly intense and by a workforce that was often portrayed as yobbo "poofter bashers". Then in June 1973, when the Professorial Board at Sydney University blocked a proposal for a women's studies course, students approached the BLF which announced a ban on all further construction work on the campus. Yet again they won.

The Green Bans to save working-class housing, heritage buildings and parkland, for which the BLF became most famous, did not then come from nowhere. They flowed from growing industrial confidence and an assertion that workers are not robots toiling at the whim of profit-driven developers. The workers believed that they should have a clear say over what they built in the interests of the broader working class. They sought to tame the concrete jungle. As one young labourer, Dave Shaw – who had been on the CPA Sydney District Committee before resigning because of the CPA's rightward drift to join the International Socialists – wrote:

> The BLF leadership cultivated a remarkable militancy among the workers, smashing down scab work, work-ins, occupations like the occupation of the Hilton site in George Street. We saw the results

---

42. Burgmann and Burgmann 1999, p53.

they got with these tactics, and the way they encouraged the workers to take their own initiatives.

It was easy for me to support the green bans. The spectacular events that accompanied them, the occupations, the arrests, the demonstrations, all of this captured my imagination and I'm sure they captured the imagination of a lot of other workers.

At that time a majority of the membership supported the green bans, there's no doubt about that. Not just because they supported the principle, but also because at that time the industry was booming, and you could ban jobs left, right and centre, because you could always go and get a job somewhere down the road.

Another thing that impressed me was that the CPA made an attempt to bring women into the industry. There can be no doubt that on many jobs some of the workers voted in favour of it for sexist reasons: that it would be "great to have a sheila on the job", but nevertheless I think that it did a lot to break down the myth that women can't do hard physical work.[43]

In NSW there were about 60 women BLs. In Victoria under Gallagher there was only one, Sandra Zurbo, a supporter of the rank and file opposition to the Maoist leadership that published a broadsheet, *On Site*. Zurbo pointed out that Gallagher's officials "refused to use the tactic that was used in NSW, of getting women to go on the job, talk to the workers there, and have a struggle on the job".[44] The Maoists, and in particular Gallagher's cohorts, were renowned for gross homophobia and sexism. Their starkly different attitude to women's rights compared to that of the NSW BLF was reflected in the actions of Gallagher's ally, Queensland BLF Secretary Vince Dobinson. Dobinson notoriously gave the order: "OK boys, rip it down" when a Women's Liberation banner was raised at the 1975 Brisbane May Day march.[45]

The Green Ban movement really got underway in June 1971 when a Hunter's Hill resident action group approached

43. Shaw 1976, p9.
44. Stone 1975, p3.
45. Slater 1975, p6.

the BLF to save Kelly's Bush as open public space. The union wholeheartedly backed them. When developer AV Jennings threatened to use scab labour on the site, workers on another Jennings site sent this message: "If you attempt to build on Kelly's Bush, even if there is the loss of one tree, this half-completed building will remain so forever, as a monument to Kelly's Bush".[46] Kelly's Bush was saved!

In 1972 Jack Mundey declared:

> Yes, we want to build. However, we prefer to build urgently needed hospitals, schools, other public utilities, high-quality flats, units and houses, provided they are designed with adequate concern for the environment, than to build ugly unimaginative architecturally bankrupt blocks of concrete and glass offices... Though we want all our members employed, we will not just become robots directed by developer-builders who value the dollar at the expense of the environment. More and more, we are going to determine which buildings we will build.[47]

Major Green Ban battles included The Rocks, where a bitterly fought ban that included many arrests of protesting residents and workers saved the oldest European-built buildings in Australia and housing for low-income workers. In Woolloomooloo, working-class housing was again saved. Another flashpoint was Victoria St, Kings Cross, where the Green Ban on an important area of working-class housing was lifted after federal intervention by Gallagher, who was in cahoots with, and very likely funded by, gangster developer Frank Theeman.

By 1975 the bans had stalled development worth $5 billion at mid-1970s prices.[48] The Master Builders Association (MBA), which well before the Green Ban period was out to get the NSW BLF, piled the pressure on Gallagher's federal leadership

---

46. Burgmann and Burgmann 2011.
47. Thomas 1973, pp56-57.
48. Burgmann and Burgmann, 2011.

to destroy them. NSW Liberal Premier Robert Askin, who was close to the developers, adopted a very hard-line approach. The NSW Summary Offences Act was consistently used by bosses in industrial disputes and specifically targeted the BLF, with police arresting organisers, and on building sites physical attacks by bosses on organisers accelerated.

The BLs and the BWIU

The BWIU had adopted a militant stance in the late 1940s and was deregistered in 1948 for striking in defiance of arbitration. In 1952 right-wing Groupers organised a split to form the Amalgamated Society of Carpenters and Joiners (ASC&J) which weakened the BWIU's industrial position. The impact was to help push the BWIU into a more conservative mould. According to Jack Mundey the BWIU had to undertake not to engage in militant action in order to regain registration, which was not obtained until September 1962. It placed an emphasis on alliances with various right-wing unions in the industry. Indeed a deal was done between the left- and right-wing unions in NSW construction that they would not interfere in each other's affairs.

The BWIU operated in a very top-down way, with a strong bureaucratic machine dominated by its secretary Pat Clancy, a leading CPA and subsequently SPA member. Clancy did not hold a mass meeting of construction workers for 14 years. Jack Mundey explained that in his early years "I was in the same party as Clancy and went along with the thinking of that period... which was ideologically Stalinist". He believed that "for the first years [the BLF] tended to be a pretty much BWIU-advised show".[49]

In the 1950s and '60s the CPA building branch, which brought together 40-50 CPA members across the various unions in the industry, was dominated by the BWIU. Clancy was the key figure, backed up by other BWIU officials and Sid Vaughan from

49. Burgmann 1981, pxxiv.

the Painters Union. According to BLF leader Joe Owens Clancy was for a whole period respected by the "junior militants" in the BLF and regarded as "almost a father figure".[50] Initially there was a broad consensus in the building branch, and after the defeat of the old right-wing BLF leadership the BWIU provided the BLF with facilities and office space. However as the BLF became more militant, relations sharply deteriorated. The BWIU detested the organised vigilante groups that were used to destroy scab building work. As Mundey commented, "conservative tradesmen's leaders threw up their hands in horror at the 'terrible crime' of a few scab-built walls being pushed over".[51]

Mundey explained:

> Our style was to encourage rank and filers to show their initiative while at the same time remembering that unity was important. We didn't pose one argument against the other. You want unity at the top but more importantly you want action by workers down below... We were allowing shop committees and area strike committees to be set up...to make decisions affecting their own area. The BWIU saw anything like this as a challenge to their own centralised leadership.[52]

Reflecting the growing tensions in April 1971 the BLF was kicked out of the offices they shared in the BWIU's Vine House. The BWIU went on to play a crucial role in isolating the BLF and allowing Norm Gallagher and the bosses to crush it.

Gallagher and the Maoists

A section of the CPA's hard-core Stalinist leadership had never liked Russian leader Nikita Khrushchev's denunciations of Stalin and the embrace of peaceful coexistence with the West. In the late 1950s Victorian CPA leader Ted Hill, the epitome of a ruthless and paranoid Stalinist bureaucrat, rallied support for

---

50. Burgmann 1981, piv.
51. Burgmann and Burgmann, 1999, p51.
52. Burgmann and Burgmann, 1998, p255.

the Chinese CP "on a platform of greater militancy, hostility to reformism and a more 'balanced' appraisal of Stalin".[53]

The Maoists split in 1963 to form the Communist Party of Australia (Marxist Leninist) – CPA (ML). They managed to take out a number of prominent union leaders. However, despite the CPA (ML)'s radical rhetoric, the practice of Maoist union officials such as Clarrie O'Shea of the Tramways Union and Paddy Malone of the BLF proved to be no more militant than that of the CPA union bureaucrats. Malone, a CPA (ML) Central Committee member, had been Victorian BLF secretary since 1941 and remained in office for almost 30 years. Under Malone's leadership the BLF was a fairly conventional bureaucratic affair, though not the worst of the Stalinist-controlled unions. It remained moderately militant, though far from outstandingly so.

Malone had some influence among BLs in the Sydney Rank and File Committee and the Maoists managed to build a small presence there. According to Les Robinson, who was installed by Gallagher as NSW BLF secretary at the time of intervention, the split of the "China-liners" from the NSW leadership in 1961-63 was caused mainly by objections to Mick McNamara's secretaryship: "we didn't oppose Jack [Mundey], my argument was that Jack should take over the leadership".[54]

The thoroughly unscrupulous Norm Gallagher, also a leading figure in the CPA (ML), took over as secretary from Malone in 1970. Under Gallagher the Victorian BLF became increasingly authoritarian and intolerant of dissent. Gallagher was pretty much a lifelong union bureaucrat, having become a full-time organiser as early as 1952. Gallagher was prepared to engage in militant tactics when it suited his empire-build-ing ambitions, but was also notorious for cutting deals with favoured bosses.

---

53. O'Lincoln 1985, p101.
54. Burgmann 1981, pxiv.

Confronting the question of union bureaucracy

The NSW BLF made a concerted attempt to confront the question of union bureaucracy and the political conservatism that went with it. As Mundey put it:

> Quite unlike many bureaucratic union leaderships...[t]he [BLF] leadership aims for "total involvement" in decision making by the membership. We are opposed to "top" decision making without reference to the membership.

He declared himself "very critical of the union movement as a whole for its tendency for people in top positions to become entrenched" and to use union positions "as stepping stones to some political position".[55] This was a significant step forward and a starkly different approach to every other section of the union movement.

From 1968 onwards they introduced major changes to democratise the union, including the frequent use of mass stop-work meetings, the tying of officials' wages to the BLF award, limited tenure of office for officials, temporary organisers with a considerable number of members rotating through these positions, an emphasis on job autonomy, the opening of union executive meetings to all members, and the non-payment of officials during industry-wide strikes. Leaving aside the specific value of some of these reforms, the overall orientation was an enormously positive one that challenged the rest of the union movement. These democratic reforms served to empower the rank and file and limit the ability of the union leadership to flout the wishes of members. Nonetheless they did not resolve the fundamental question of the inherent limitations of trade unions under capitalism when it came to the struggle for socialism.

Unions are institutions that bargain about the rate of exploitation of the working class within the bounds of

---

55. Burgmann and Burgmann 1999, pp49-50.

capitalism. They fight for a larger slice of the pie, not the whole bakery. Moreover, overwhelmingly they organise and bargain on behalf of specific sectional groups of workers, not the class as a whole. They are not and cannot be revolutionary organisations that can unite the mass of workers and the oppressed and potential allies from intermediary social layers, such as students, in the struggle to overthrow capitalism. To be effective unions need to organise the bulk of workers in any specific industry; the passive and conservative as well as the committed activists and everyone in between. Unions are inevitably forced to make concessions to the lowest common denominator. This severely undermines the ability of unions to play a genuinely revolutionary role. As Jack Mundey noted, even in the case of a radical union like the NSW BLF, most of its members were straightforward Labor voters, not revolutionaries.[56] Various attempts by syndicalists to transform unions into revolutionary instruments to lead the struggle to overthrow capitalism have always failed. Only a revolutionary socialist party that organises the most class-conscious workers into a cohered fighting force can effectively play that leadership role.

The NSW BLF essentially adopted a quasi-syndicalist approach, epitomised by the arguments of its most dynamic leader Jack Mundey, who downplayed the importance of a revolutionary party: "this craziness about vanguard parties having all the knowledge... Union struggles can play the biggest part".[57] This undoubtedly was in part a reaction against the political weaknesses of the CPA, the party Mundey was to remain a member of until its dismal end, despite his own strongly held anti-Stalinist views. It also reflected an understandable negative reaction on his part against the super-heated rhetoric of various tiny sectarian groups that ridiculously posed as already being "the vanguard" of the working class.

The other limitation was that the leading BLF militants

---

56. O'Lincoln 1985, p198.
57. Burgmann and Burgmann 1999, p56.

did not develop a thorough-going analysis of the social role of the union bureaucracy as a mediating layer between capital and labour. They fought for rank and file democracy and opposed the conservative bureaucratic role that union officials generally played. However they did not fully recognise that in advanced capitalist societies the trade union bureaucracy was a thoroughly counter-revolutionary social layer which would act as a bulwark in the defence of capitalist rule in the face of any concerted working class offensive. One consequence of this was that they underestimated the enemy that they were up against. They did not fully appreciate that they had thrown down a decisive challenge to the rest of the union bureaucracy which would inevitably move to crush them. The only road forward was for the BLF leadership to initiate the building of a rank and file movement across the whole of industry to lead the class struggle independently of the union bureaucracy. They were held back from implementing such a revolutionary orientation in part because of the continuing influence of the Communist Party's reformist politics. Only a sharp break by the BLF militants from the CPA and an attempt to rally the radical forces outside its ranks in a new revolutionary party offered any hope of a road forward.

Gallagher's intervention

With the full weight of the building bosses behind him, Gallagher arrived in Sydney on 12 October 1974 and ensconced himself on a whole floor of the Hyde Park Plaza Hotel. Determined to crush his arch-rival, Gallagher brought with him a legion of armed thugs funded by the bosses to act as organisers, including Scotch College-educated student Maoist and future Tasmanian Labor premier Jim Bacon.

Gallagher set up a new federal BLF branch to replace the NSW BLF. On 18 October leading builder EA Watts sacked BLs who refused to take out the federal union ticket. Dillinghams and other bosses soon followed suit.[58] Knowing that under Gallagher the bosses would have open slather, an MBA circular to its members declared that the MBA "actively encourages commencement of work on projects subject to illegal bans".[59] A long list of NSW officials and prominent militants were summarily expelled for life from the BLF.

The NSW branch was a serious danger to Gallagher's control over the BLF nationally. Because of the scale of the Sydney building boom, by 1974 the NSW BLF made up nearly half the union's national membership. Jack Mundey, thanks to the intense media coverage of the BLF's exploits, was massively better known around the country than Gallagher and posed a real threat in any election for federal secretary. The NSW BLF was also a major impediment to Gallagher in his empire-building attempts to take on the BWIU and become the dominant force among building industry unions. There was also a sharp ideological divide between the radical democratic class-struggle politics of the NSW BLF and Gallagher's top-down Stalinist approach and strident Australian nationalism.

As well, Gallagher was under growing pressure from bosses outraged at the impact the ongoing militancy in NSW was having on their profits. The bosses may not have loved Gallagher – though he was close to some of them such as Bruno Grollo and EA Watts – but they very much saw him as a lesser evil to Mundey and co. As early as 1972 there were concerted calls by the NSW MBA for the deregistration of the BLF, but at that point Gallagher held off moving against the NSW branch, concerned that the boom in the industry and the confidence that gave the rank and file would mean he would face a difficult, drawn-out fight.

In October 1973 the NSW BLF leadership forces had a convincing election victory, with Joe Owens replacing Mundey, who stood down under the limited tenure rule, as secretary and

---

58. Boyd 1991, p11.
59. Burgmann and Burgmann 1998, p269.

Bob Pringle elected president. By a margin of two to one they defeated a Maoist pro-Gallagher opposition (John McNamara, Ron Donoghue and Joe Ferguson) whose platform criticised many of the Green Bans.

In June 1974 the bosses had the courts deregister the BLF federally in an attempt to force Gallagher's hand. This was the tipping point. The bosses made it clear to Gallagher that if he disposed of the NSW branch and rolled back the Green Bans, the BLF would be re-registered federally without any fuss. That is precisely what happened in October 1976.

There was concerted opposition to Gallagher's intervention. As Dave Shaw explained, Gallagher had no support from the rank and file in Sydney. There were virtual riots when his organisers arrived:

> On one of the Concrete Constructions jobs 35 BLs got arrested when they occupied the site in protest at the Gallagher forces. On Qantas, there was a riot in Jamison Street.
>
> At the Martin Place Eastern Suburbs Railway site, a couple of Gallagher's new organisers were in the sheds talking to the boss. All the workers marched up from Qantas and joined the workers at Martin Place. They surrounded the shed, and the organisers could not get out. In the end they had to back a paddy wagon up to the shed to get them out.[60]

A mass meeting of 1,500 BLs voted unanimously to reject Gallagher's takeover. Gallagher was invited to address the meeting but refused, saying it was stacked with "residents and poofters".[61] Intervention was timed to coincide with the annual dues renewal period, but in the first three weeks the NSW BLF signed up 7,000 members while Gallagher netted less than 1,000. But despite this defiance and in the face of intimidation – arrests and police attacks combined with widespread victimisation and sackings by the bosses – the BLs were

---

60. Shaw 1976, p9.
61. Burgmann and Burgmann 1998, p269.

defeated. On Monday 24 March 1975, on the recommendation of the Owens and Pringle leadership, a mass meeting of BLs voted to join Gallagher's federal branch and continue the fight from within. Opinion is divided among the militants about whether this was the correct approach, but many felt that by this stage defeat was inevitable. There were numerous resignations from the CPA over its failure to fully mobilise to defend the BLF.

The defeat led to the severe demoralisation of good militants, with many denied union tickets by Gallagher or victimised by the bosses and driven out of the industry. A number of serious militants adopted an anti-political standpoint or retreated into a narrow syndicalism or dropped out of activity disillusioned.

Gallagher claimed, of course, to support "the principle" of Green Bans. But the Gallagher-installed leadership immediately lifted a number of bans without any endorsement by the rank and file. Notoriously, one of the first Green Bans lifted was in Victoria Street at the bidding of Gallagher's thug mate Theeman, who was helping fund Gallagher's operation. In order to further shore up support from building industry bosses, Gallagher stabbed the Victorian union movement in the back by breaking ranks to lift the ban on construction of the highly polluting Newport power station.[62]

But it was not just over Green Bans that Gallagher aided the bosses. Gallagher pushed through a new award that undermined conditions on the job, including forcing workers to work in the rain with umbrellas. Body hire proliferated. Unsurprisingly, union membership fell sharply after intervention. Workers were less well placed to resist technological change and speed-up. Accidents increased and more building workers lost their lives. Dave Shaw, who was active in the ongoing rank and file resistance to Gallagher, was one of those eventually killed on the job.

With the recession in the construction industry deepening,

---

62. Griffiths 1974, p8.

the bosses went on the rampage. Fify-seven thousand construction workers – 30 percent of the national total – lost their jobs between 1973 and 1979. By 1979 there were fewer building workers than at any time in the previous 15 years.[63] Inner city construction jobs, which had been the mainstay of militancy and where thousands of workers had been gathered, were particularly badly hit.[64]

Nonetheless concerted opposition continued to the Gallagher-imposed leadership. One reflection of that was that no BLF branch meetings or mass meetings were allowed in Sydney for two years after intervention. The first open branch meeting in 1977 saw two-thirds of members present in outright opposition to the officials. The officials refused to accept any resolutions, and walked out when a motion of no confidence was moved in their leadership.[65]

The Builders Labourers for Democratic Control – the rank and file opposition group – had widespread support. Several major building sites backed it, and delegates sympathetic to it led numerous important strike campaigns on their jobs, which placed in stark relief the tame-cat leadership of the Gallagher forces. Despite continuing victimisation by the bosses and the Gallagher forces, the BLs for Democratic Control were holding meetings of 60-80 activists in 1977.

In 1978,

> after a long campaign for a democratic ballot...the BLs for Democratic Control finally went to the courts to secure an election. Their activists placed all their hopes on winning the ballot, and when Gallagher's men out-organised them, they were thoroughly demoralised.
>
> Their failure to use the election to spread their organisation, and to build any campaign other than a campaign for votes, meant that

---

63. Shaw 1979, p13.
64. For the subsequent history of the BLF and how the bosses were to turn on Gallagher see Ross 2004.
65. Owens 1977, p11.

they had nothing left to fall back upon once they had lost. Within a few months, the group had effectively collapsed.[66]

Groups of militants did regroup, for example at the Johns and Waygood ICI site in Sydney where a number of former BLF militants were concentrated together holding FIA cards. However as Dave Shaw wrote:

> In the Johns and Waygood dispute the company sacked the whole workforce. The J & W workers had fought the boss from the start of the job and won significant gains. But in the process we became isolated and were defeated.[67]

The crushing of the NSW BLF was a defeat for the whole of the then sizeable radical left. Its path-breaking achievements had been an inspiration for revolutionaries. This was strongly the case for the student movement which was still under strong far left influence. *The Battler* reported that at the 1975 Australian Union of Students (AUS) conference:

> After a fiery debate and in the face of threats and intimidation from Gallagher's supporters, AUS...came out in support of the NSW branch of the Builders Labourers' Federation in their struggle... Delegates voted decisively against a policy of non-involvement in the dispute.[68]

This actually understates the scale of the violent confrontation that occurred at the conference, which I attended as a delegate from La Trobe University. For hour after hour Maoist students rioted in an attempt to prevent socialist delegates from speaking and voting. The conference was particularly polarised as one of the Maoists, AUS office bearer Peter Galvin, was working as a Gallagher organiser on Sydney's North Shore.

---

66. Kahn 1981, p11.
67. Shaw 1979, p13.
68. *The Battler*, 15 February 1975, p3.

Why the defeat?

As *The Battler* declared at the time: "The defeat of the NSW branch of the BLs is a victory for violence, intimidation and thuggery which has no place in the labour movement".[69]

The downturn in the construction industry had put the NSW militants in a weaker position to resist Gallagher's assault. They were overwhelmed by the combined forces arrayed against them. Gallagher's thugs had the backing, not just of the employers, the government and the cops, but also Bob Hawke, then head of the ACTU, and most other union officials. The other main supposedly left-wing union in the construction industry, the Clancy-led BWIU, stood on the sidelines, effectively supporting Gallagher. Clancy and his SPA supporters spent more time denouncing the "adventurism" and "ultra-militancy" of the NSW BLF than the thuggery of the Gallagher forces.[70] However Clancy and the other SPA-aligned officials were simply more open in expressing a common sentiment among the left wing of the union bureaucracy, including many CPA officials. The reality was that the NSW BLF's democratic culture and aggressive militancy posed a challenge to their bureaucratic empires.

The NSW Federated Engine Drivers and Firemens Association of Australasia (FEDFA), led by Jack Cambourn, was the only CPA-led union to offer meaningful industrial support to the NSW BLF. FEDFA crane drivers refused to work with Gallagher ticket holders and struck for six weeks after the bosses responded by cutting their wages. But Gallagher flew in scabs from Melbourne to break their strike. Verbal support came from the NSW Teachers Federation and the Australian Telecommunications Employees' Association. However, the powerful Metalworkers Union, whose leadership included the prominent Communists Laurie Carmichael and John Halfpenny, and which had members in key sections of the

69. Griffiths 1975, p3.
70. See Building Industry Branch of the Socialist Party of Australia, n.d., for an outline of the SPA line.

construction industry, did nothing to defend their fellow party members. The right-wing Victorian CPA branch, which was far from enamoured with Mundey's militancy, did little to mobilise to defend the BLs. Indeed Victorian CPA Secretary Bernie Taft criticised the NSW BLF for "a tendency to counterpose the rank and file movement to the trade union officials".[71]

This does not mean that the NSW leadership made no mistakes. Jack Mundey stated that he "did feel at the time that the union was travelling too quickly" and that "we made an error in taking up too many social issues at the final stages...we took on too much, I think we failed to consolidate at a certain period". Tom O'Lincoln noted:

> There had been a prolonged boom, and workers were prepared to take all sorts of advanced...actions, secure in the knowledge that labour was tight. It was possible for members and leaders to get a bit giddy, and to find themselves suddenly vulnerable when the boom came to an end in 1974.[72]

According to Dave Shaw the NSW leadership was

> overwhelmed by superior force, but there had also been a neglect of organisation on the job level. Only two or three jobs in Sydney had site committees, linking BLs to the other unions... If more jobs had had them, we'd have had a better show of beating Gallagher. On the jobs that did have site committees, they pretty successfully resisted him, and have maintained their conditions.[73]

At the Qantas and Bondi Plaza sites conditions were defended and Gallagher's agents were kept at arm's length. The Bondi Plaza site committee included a delegate from each trade. Mass meetings were held weekly and they did not restrict themselves to bread-and-butter issues. Political discussions were organised every week. And when anti-migrant racism broke out, they knew

---

71. Taft 1975.
72. O'Lincoln 1985, p151.
73. Shaw 1976, p9.

how to handle it. Delegates took a solid stand against racism and for unity of all the workers. The offenders were instructed to apologise by an overwhelming vote at a mass meeting.

There had also been a longstanding failure to make a priority of building rank and file opposition groups in the other construction unions. This reflected a certain sectionalism among the BLs and a mistaken political approach coming from the CPA for a whole period, that you did not interfere in the affairs of other unions. And at the time of intervention there was a failure to make a concerted attempt to use the already mobilised rank and file BLs to go out to other workplaces and unions to argue their case and mobilise support. Nonetheless with all that said and done, Jack Mundey was entirely correct when he argued: "Yes, mistakes, but always keep in mind that had other unions displayed working class solidarity with the democratically elected NSW leadership...the 'invasion' would have certainly failed".[74] As for the charges of ultraleftism and adventurism, Pete Cockcroft put it well in a letter to *Tribune* in reply to an attack on the BLs for being too militant and not relying instead on "patient work":

> Cde. Alf Watt's "patient work" is all very well, but in no situation can that work alone lead to that qualitative leap which was at the core of the BLF's achievement.
>
> The history of the working class movement is in large part the history of groups of workers who were prepared to go out on a limb. Of course it is an error to ignore the present consciousness of workers. But it is a far more dangerous error to regard that consciousness (or rather the consciousness of the bureaucrats that exploit it), as a constant barrier which we must never transcend.[75]

---

74. O'Lincoln 1985, p152.
75. Cockcroft 1975. *Tribune*, 13 May 1975, p11.

Conclusion

There is a small chance that if the BLs had pulled back considerably, lifted many of the Green Bans and become a mediocre tame-cat union, then they could have survived. But what would have been the point of that? It is much better to give battle and be defeated than demean yourself by crawling on your belly to the powers-that-be. It is only by fighting that the working class movement has ever achieved anything. Socialist militants obviously should attempt to employ the most effective tactics. But the standard rhetoric of left officials of "boxing clever" is just code for never even putting on your gloves and getting into the ring.

One smallish union in one state, no matter how militant and how skilful its tactics, was never going to be capable on its own of indefinitely taking on and defeating the hostile array of class forces that rallied to crush the NSW BLF. It needed *active* support and solidarity from a much broader section of the working class. The potential for such solidarity definitely existed in the early 1970s. It was a period of an enormous upsurge in working-class struggle and a flowering in a number of industries of shop floor organisation to a considerable extent independent of the dead weight of the union bureaucracy. There was no shortage of militancy. The tragedy was that there was no socialist political force able and willing to cohere the many tens of thousands of rank and file militants, most of whom identified as socialists, in the factories, the mines, the wharves and the schools as well as the building sites, into an organised fighting force.

The Communist Party, which many of the best BLF militants joined, was singularly incapable of that task. The CPA, easily the largest force on the left at the time, had jettisoned some of its worst Stalinist baggage and briefly shifted leftwards. However, it was anything but a coherent, interventionist revolutionary party. It still contained a layer of entrenched union bureaucrats wedded to reformism and a cohort of middle-class and student members who were little more than radical liberals. There was no way it could mobilise a fighting cross-industry rank and file movement to defend the BLF and advance the broader class struggle. The new revolutionary socialist groups that had emerged out of the late sixties radical upsurge simply lacked the forces to fill the breach. We can't afford to let that happen next time round.

So the inspiring militants of the NSW BLF went down to defeat; but they left a powerful legacy. They showed what workers are capable of when they organise and stand up for their class interests and reach out in solidarity to all the oppressed. That approach can lay the basis for a very different world. And as I wrote in *Red Flag* at the time of Jack Mundey's death:

> The fighting spirit of the BLF in Jack Mundey's heyday is something desperately needed in today's economic crisis with the bosses going for the jugular to destroy wages and conditions. Decades of union bureaucrats falling over backwards to compromise with the bosses and suck up to the ALP have got us nowhere. We need to organise to turn the tide.[76]

References

Adams, Paul Robert 2010, *The Best Hated Man in Australia. The life and death of Percy Brookfield 1875-1921*, Puncher & Wattmann.

Armstrong, Mick 2013, "Socialist trade union strategy in the Bolshevik era", *Marxist Left Review*, 6, Winter. https://marxistleftreview.org/articles/socialist-trade-union-strategy-in-the-bolshevik-era/.

Armstrong, Mick 2020, "What's the legacy of Jack Mundey, union militant?", *Red Flag*, 11 May. https://redflag.org.au/index.php/node/7175.

Boyd, Brian 1991, *Inside the BLF*, Ocean Press.

Bramble, Tom 2008, *Trade Unionism in Australia. A history from flood to ebb tide*, Cambridge University Press.

---

76. Armstrong 2020.

Building Industry Branch of the Socialist Party of Australia, n.d., *Six Turbulent Years: Lessons from the rise and fall of the NSW Builders Labourers' leadership and building industry struggles 1968-75*.

Burgmann, Meredith 1981, *A New Concept of Unionism: the New South Wales Builders Labourers' Federation 1970-1974*, PhD thesis, Macquarie University.

Burgmann, Meredith and Verity Burgmann 1998, *Green Bans, Red Union. Environmental activism and the New South Wales Builders Labourers Federation*, UNSW Press.

Burgmann, Meredith and Verity Burgmann 1999, "'A rare shift in public thinking': Jack Mundey and the New South Wales Builders Labourers' Federation", *Labour History*, 77.

Burgmann, Meredith and Verity Burgmann 2011, "Green Bans Movement", https://dictionaryofsydney.org/entry/green_bans_movement.

Cliff, Tony and Donny Gluckstein 1986, *Marxism and Trade Union Struggle. The General Strike of 1926*, Bookmarks.

Cockcroft, Peter 1975, letter to *Tribune*, 13 May.

Davidson, Alastair 1969, *The Communist Party of Australia. A short history*, Hoover Institution Press.

Griffiths, Phil 1974, "Glory Without Power", *The Battler*, 16 November. http://www.reasoninrevolt.net.au/objects/pdf/d0117.pdf.

Griffiths, Phil 1975, "Feds smash NSW union", *The Battler*, 5 April. http://www.reasoninrevolt.net.au/objects/pdf/d0118.pdf.

Kahn, Alec 1981, "The industrial struggle since 1975. The Fraser Years", *International Socialist*, 11, Autumn. http://www.reasoninrevolt.net.au/objects/pdf/d0514.pdf.

Kennedy, Brian 1978, *Silver, Sin and Sixpenny Ale. A social history of Broken Hill 1883-1921*, Melbourne University Press.

Mallory, Greg 2005, *Uncharted Waters: Social responsibility in Australian trade unions*, self-published.

Martin, Roderick 1969, *Communism and the British Trade Unions 1924-1933. A study of the National Minority Movement*, Clarendon Press.

Mundey, Jack 1981, *Green Bans & Beyond*, Angus & Robertson.

O'Lincoln, Tom 1985, *Into the Mainstream. The decline of Australian Communism*, Stained Wattle Press.

Owens, Joe 1977, "The NSW BLF – strangled by officials", letter to *The Battler*, 28 May. http://www.reasoninrevolt.net.au/objects/pdf/d0120.pdf.

Ross, Liz 2004, *Dare to Struggle, Dare to Win! Builders Labourers fight deregistration, 1981-94*, Vulgar Press.

Shaw, David 1976, "Why I am joining the International Socialists", *The Battler*, 15 December. http://www.reasoninrevolt.net.au/objects/pdf/d0119.pdf.

Shaw, David 1979, "Crisis in the concrete jungle", *International Socialist*, 8, Autumn. http://www.reasoninrevolt.net.au/objects/pdf/d0511.pdf.

Sheldon, Peter 1988, "Job Control for Workers' Health: the 1908 Sydney Rockchoppers' Strike", *Labour History*, 55, November.

Slater, Joyce 1975, "March ban fails", *Tribune*, 13 May.

Stone, Janey 1975, "It's MY bloody union card and I want the job!", interview with Sandra Zurbo, *The Battler*, 15 February. http://www.reasoninrevolt. net.au/objects/pdf/d0118.pdf.

Taft, Bernie 1975, "On the Defeat of the NSW Builders' Laborers [sic]", http:// surplusvalue.org.au/McQueen/BLF/documents/blf_docs_blf_nsw_ defeat.html.

The Battler, 1975, "Students Oppose Scab Intervention" (no author), 15 February. http://www.reasoninrevolt.net.au/objects/pdf/d0118.pdf.

Thomas, Pete 1973, *Taming the concrete jungle. The Builders Labourers' story*, NSW branch of the Australian Building Construction Employees & Builders Labourers' Federation.

True, Paul 1995, *Tales of the BLF...Rolling the Right!*, Militant International Publications.

Turner, Ian 1978, *In Union is Strength. A history of trade unions in Australia 1788-1978*, second edition, Nelson.

Wood, Katie 2013, "Fighting anti-union laws: the Clarrie O'Shea strikes", *Marxist Left Review*, 5, Summer. https://marxistleftreview.org/articles/ fighting-anti-union-laws-the-clarrie-oshea-strikes/.

Woodhouse, Michael and Brian Pearce 1975, *Essays on the History of Communism in Britain*, New Park.

DIANE FIELDES AND JORDAN HUMPHREYS[1]

NTEU Fightback: Rank-and-file rebellion in a most unlikely union

Diane Fieldes has been active since the early 1970s in many campaigns including those for Indigenous and refugee rights. She has written about a range of working class struggles such as the struggle for equal pay.

Jordan Humphreys is a socialist activist in Sydney and a regular contributor to the *Marxist Left Review*.

THE COVID-19 PANDEMIC has fundamentally transformed the university sector. On one hand, campuses have experienced a sharp fall in revenue, triggering a financial crisis, with huge cuts to wages, jobs and courses on the cards. At the same time, the sector has seen an unprecedented surge of rank and file union activity that has achieved some important, if tentative, wins. This article will explore the issues raised by the struggle so far, with the hope of arming a new layer of activists with the arguments they need to carry on the fight, which will undoubtedly extend for years to come.

The sector is expected to lose up to $19 billion over the next three years, primarily due to a sharp drop in international student enrolments.[2] But this crisis didn't come out of the blue. University workers have been under pressure since Labor's introduction of student fees in 1989. Since then, both Labor and Coalition governments have slashed federal funding per student. Students now graduate with large debts. Meanwhile, vice-chancellors have expanded revenue by enrolling hundreds

---

1. This article could not have been written without the tireless work of the members of the Socialist Alternative NTEU caucus and SA industrial organiser Jerome Small in every aspect of the fightback in the NTEU.
2. Hurley 2020.

of thousands of overseas students who pay high up-front fees. University bosses have increasingly looked to employ low-paid and insecure casual and contract workers to cut costs in their enterprises. Less than half of universities' "full-time equivalent" workers have secure ongoing positions and more than half of all teaching is done by casual staff. As an immediate response to the crisis, Australian vice-chancellors have already laid off thousands, and increased the workloads of the workers who remain.[3]

Shamefully, the top officials of the National Tertiary Education Union (NTEU) responded by surrendering without a fight. In an email to members on 8 April, the NTEU general secretary Matt McGowan wrote: "To protect jobs, we may need to consider measures that we would never normally consider. These may include deferral of pay rises, providing the ability to direct taking of leave, or other cost saving measures. Any changes must be temporary and proportional to the loss at each university".[4] Later the NTEU officials announced a "national jobs protection framework" (JPF or "the framework" in what follows) to offer to university managements before members heard anything about it. It involved cuts to wages and conditions in exchange for nebulous and unenforceable undertakings about saving jobs.

Matt McGowan explained the underlying rationale behind the framework at a Q&A session at RMIT on 25 May: that the framework would give the union

> a form of authority that it hasn't had in over three decades. A national framework where the union is at the centre... We've not had that sort of authority in decades. And this will significantly improve the union's ability to impact on the future structure and direction of the sector. I'm not saying that's all written into the agreement, that's not. That's a comment about the way in which

---

3. Barrigos 2013, Kuhn and Hynes 2020, Long 2018.
4. Torlakovic and Kuhn 2020a.

this dynamic can play out, if we play our cards right and we do what needs to be done.

The NTEU officials were thus prepared to sacrifice their members' livelihoods for a seat at the table in implementing the cuts.

This approach won the support of Liberal education minister Dan Tehan, who found time between raising student fees and gutting government funding to praise the "very good discussions going on at the moment between the university sector and the NTEU".[5]

Yet just two months later, the national framework was dead in the water. A rank and file rebellion led by a coordinated network of activists across the country destroyed the officials' hopes for a national concessional agreement. The campaign introduced grassroots activism into workplaces where it has been mostly lacking, as lively meetings of hundreds of staff proliferated across a sector with a weak history of union activism. The campaign posed political issues about the purpose of unions; do they exist to help manage the "industry" alongside bosses, or should they oppose attacks on members at all costs?[6] As well, the role of socialists in such a fight was sharply posed, given the long history of ex-revolutionaries climbing the rungs of the NTEU bureaucracy.[7]

None of these political questions are unique to the NTEU. A severe crisis such as that revealed by the consequences of the COVID-19 pandemic throws everything in society into sharp relief. Despite decades of defeat and retreat from Australia's union movement, sections of unionised workers, including most of the public sector like university workers, have maintained above-minimum wages and conditions. All of these entitlements are now under threat. This makes the resistance of NTEU members to the current attacks important to

5. Tehan 2020.
6. Bramble 2018.
7. Wood and Torlakovic 2020.

all workers. Further, despite the initial victory, union officials have not given up on the class collaboration that underlies their strategy, and have successfully pushed through versions of the agreement at a local level. It is yet to be seen how the workers respond to this new and more difficult situation.

The nature of the NTEU

Much of what follows is relevant to the class struggle in any union but there are a number of features of the NTEU that make the fightback within it somewhat surprising. To begin with, the union continues to suffer from its pre-history as a series of academic staff associations that did not see themselves as part of the union movement. This tradition, as well as the individ- ualising effect of academic work – with personal endeavour rather than collective struggle as the road to better pay – have not been conducive to union consciousness.[8] Compounding these issues is the fact that a majority of the members are still academics rather than professional and technical staff, who tend to have less idealist and middle-class conceptions about the university and their role within it. While there is a tendency in every union to identify with the industry in which it operates, this is stronger in the NTEU than most: when heads of depart- ments, deans and even vice-chancellors can be members, it is no wonder that there is a greater propensity to see the union as a "partner" in the well-being of the sector.

Union density is no better than the abysmally low average across all workplaces, and the NTEU's delegate structure is weak. Union elections are more often than not uncontested for lack of candidates. The elected officials have no real base of support and little connection to the campuses, beyond the organisers and branch leaderships. One way in which this can be seen is the top officials' reliance on the union machine of paid organisers and elected officials to get the vote out against the rank and file opposition – there is little organic loyalty

8. O'Brien 2015.

or commitment to the union leadership to be found among workers.

In other ways, the sector looks a lot like many others. Decades of federal government underfunding and corporatisation of management have resulted in unsustainable increases in workloads and stress; massive casualisation and constant restructures and redundancies have made job security a rarity even for those on continuing contracts.

Neoliberal education

Having been deliberately starved of government funding despite a long-term boom in enrolments, the sector evolved to depend on overcharging hundreds of thousands of international students in order to make its profits. The industry is now "broke" because of the deliberate policy of successive governments. Australia's university sector has been redesigned to manufacture education for export. Prior to the pandemic, international student fees made up around a quarter of the university sector's revenue.[9] As successive governments have cut university funding, universities have been encouraged to enrol increasing numbers of international students to make up the shortfall. Between 2008 and 2017, revenues from fee-paying overseas students increased from nearly $19 billion to $32 billion. At the end of 2019, there were over 200,000 Chinese international students in Australia (28 percent of the overall international student population). Education services for international students are Australia's third-largest export earner, after iron ore and coal.[10]

There is also a long-term trend in Australian higher education, pursued by both Labor and Liberal governments, to better align higher education with the needs of big business. Since 1989, when a Labor government introduced student fees, higher education participation rates have more than doubled.

9. Ferguson and Sherrell, 2019.
10. Taylor 2020.

Increasingly, employers expect graduates to have a skill set tailored to business needs. Recently announced increases in student fees for humanities subjects, while reducing those for science and technology, teaching, nursing and other subjects supposed to produce so-called "job-ready" graduates, continue this trend.

The vulnerability of the existing set-up has been exposed by the global pandemic, which means that university managers are now facing losses in the hundreds of millions of dollars. Some have threatened to close entire universities unless harsh attacks on jobs, wages and working conditions are pushed through. Universities Australia chairwoman Deborah Terry told the ABC in April that she estimated 21,000 university jobs would go within six months.[11]

The government has refused to provide more than token amounts in assistance to the sector. It has made sure university workers at public universities are ineligible for the JobKeeper scheme, though it was happy to subsidise the private universities. The government's agenda cannot be understood as many commentators do by reference to culture wars. Instead they see an opportunity to continue the process of eroding the relatively good conditions enjoyed by an important public sector workforce, and they hope it will be an example that will spread. University bosses want to undermine wage rates, hours and other legally enforceable conditions in enterprise agreements. So university managers everywhere are taking advantage of the situation to attack their workforces.

Bureaucratic betrayal

In an email to staff at La Trobe university, vice-chancellor John Dewar asked for voluntary contributions to help cover the revenue shortfall, but also noted that, "We cannot guarantee these measures will be enough to prevent...stand down [sic]

11. Duffy 2020.

or even forced redundancies".[12] This gives the lie to the NTEU officials' argument that concessions will save jobs. As Dewar wrote, there are no guarantees that will be the case. Instead, vice-chancellors will take what the officials have offered on a platter and proceed with further redundancies and stand-downs. The experience at UNSW is indicative, with a massive 493 job cuts announced in July, despite the fact that hundreds of staff had already agreed to cut their hours and thus their pay by an exorbitant 20 percent, under the misguided apprehension that this would save jobs. In a crisis, the ruling class will be ruthless. Prime Minister Scott Morrison's early waffle about "no blue teams versus red teams...no more unions versus bosses. There are just Australians now, that's all that matters. An Australian national interest and all Australians working together" is a cynical lie.[13] It is their class alone that benefits from the idea that there is a common interest between workers and bosses.

By the end of June the hospitality and clerical unions had already conceded or even co-sponsored concessionary deals that gave up key workplace rights for their members. At the national level ACTU secretary Sally McManus has promoted this class-collaborationist line. In an interview with the ABC's *Insiders* program on 5 April, she praised the government's proposed $130 billion JobKeeper wage subsidy.[14] Having spent the early months of the pandemic in daily meetings with industrial relations minister Christian Porter, McManus went a step further in May, indicating she was willing to enter into a new Accord-style agreement to reform the industrial relations system, sitting down with employer association representatives to come up with changes. The joint union-management-sponsored attack on enterprise agreement conditions in higher education has become the most high-profile example

---

12. Ross 2020.
13. Morrison 2020.
14. McManus 2020.

of this trend not because it is unique, but because it has faced substantial resistance.

All of this is nothing new. The branding "Accord 2.0" reflects the roots of this approach in the original Prices and Incomes Accord struck between the ACTU and the Hawke Labor government in the 1980s. It involved the unions accepting pay cuts in return for vague and unenforceable commitments by the government around job creation and consultation with the union leaders. Rather than demanding government funding and higher corporate taxes to fund welfare, education and healthcare, the Accord took money out of workers' pockets in order to invest in the "social wage". This process was hugely successful, from the point of view of the bosses. The proportion of GDP going to workers dropped more in Australia than in the UK and US, despite Thatcher's and Reagan's best efforts. Worse, the Accord destroyed union militancy by promoting the idea of unions as partners with bosses rather than their enemies. Militant unionists, branches and entire unions were isolated and destroyed if they dared to resist the new orthodoxy – not by the bosses and the government – but by other unions. This set the stage for the tame-cat unionism that has predominated ever since.

Under the Accord the role of union leaders became one of preventing strikes and pacifying workers. The result was a drastic decline in union membership and the level of industrial action. In the 1970s, more than half the workforce were union members. Today, fewer than 13 percent are. Industrial action has collapsed from an annual average of 3,146,000 days on strike in the 1970s, in a population of about 13.2 million, to just 145,000 in the 2010s, in a population of 25.5 million. The political culture and norms of the union movement were transformed as the Accord undermined the autonomy, self-confidence and militancy of unions' workplace organisations and entrenched traditions of deferring to leaders and the ALP.[15]

15. Bramble 2018, O'Shea 2020.

The NTEU officials are drawing from the same playbook. A briefing provided to national councillors in April boasted that there would be "a strong union role in managing the introduction of any cost-saving measures", much of which will be made through trashing existing enterprise agreements. At stake here is not simply the union members' wages and conditions, as important as that is. It is the very basis of unionism, its goals and tasks. The idea that union representatives will be equals on "implementation committees" with management to work out what cuts to make to members' conditions and wages in line with this anti-union government's agenda sounds more like the propaganda of *1984* than a union agenda. It can only neuter members' ability to fight and further undermine the very basis of unionism.[16]

In any union, the officials are under pressure from their members below, who want to defend and improve wages and conditions, and from employers and governments above, who want to maximise profits and the economic growth it generates. Consequently, as British Marxists Tony Cliff and Donny Gluckstein argued: "At all decisive moments the union bureaucracy is bound to side with the state, but in the meantime it vacillates".[17] The pressure from above has been intensified by the COVID-19 crisis. Nonetheless, the rank and file revolt in the NTEU that subsequently unfolded shows that resistance from below is possible. It can establish and expand workers' organisation independent of the officials, and with it their sense of solidarity within and across workplaces. Largely due to opposition from their own members, the attempt by the left officials in the NTEU to establish their wage-cutting framework across the industry did not succeed, unlike the original Accord.

---

16. Wood 2020a.
17. Cliff and Gluckstein 1986.

The fightback

Within a few hours of receiving the email from general secretary McGowan on 8 April, revealing the monumental sell-out members faced, two Socialist Alternative NTEU members had written a response published on the *Red Flag* website, arguing that giving away pay and conditions will not save jobs and only undermine the union. They pointed out that union leaders representing workers in sectors like clerical and hospitality had already negotiated award changes and that in exchange they'd got nothing but unenforceable promises of job security. The same was true of the deal proposed by the NTEU officials.[18] The following day, Socialist Alternative NTEU members met to plan an initial response and build resistance. By the evening they were contacting other union activists with an *NTEU Fightback – No Concessions* sign-on statement.

Starting with a few dozen socialists, the NTEU Fightback group connected networks on campuses across Australia, including forging national links where none had existed before. The local area, campus and national "vote no" meetings were sizeable, attracting hundreds of people who rarely come to union meetings and activating many who had attended only passively in the past. Dozens of local area meetings took place across campuses to discuss what was wrong with the framework and its political implications for the sector. With the whole union apparatus against the No campaign, rank and file members had to sit down with a list of names, map their campus and figure out how to win the No vote, how to shore up the waverers and how to refute the officials' lie that cuts in wages or conditions will save jobs. Most importantly, they had to build up workplace networks of activists, the essential foundations for union strength, through meetings and individual discussions. Central to this was setting up an *NTEU Fightback – No Concessions* Facebook page and website, which provided

---

18. Torlakovic and Kuhn 2020a.

regular, sometimes daily, emails to keep members informed, helped coordinate the fight against concessions and issued leaflets explaining the situation and criticisms of what was known about the officials' proposals.[19] Hundreds of members were drawn to union branch meetings, which became scenes of furious discussion and debate – when they weren't suppressed by officials.

The strategy of making concessions on hard-won wages and conditions, especially without mounting a fight, ignited fierce debate in the union. At the University of Sydney on Thursday 9 April, rank and file members overwhelmingly censured the NTEU's national executive for its willing collaboration in undermining the members' rights. The motion was carried 117 to 2. Local officials had refused to put the motion on the agenda for the meeting, so Alma Torlakovic moved it from the floor. Censure of national union leaders is rare, but activists at Sydney University had the confidence to take this step because of their unique local experiences. Industrial actions on that campus have been stronger than elsewhere, with more serious picketing and strike action deployed during enterprise bargaining negotiations in 2013 and 2017. As well, Alma Torlakovic in particular has a history of organising struggles aiming to defend and extend conditions between bargaining periods, notably including some sizeable demonstrations. The conjunction of this union work with a relatively strong campus left has left a legacy, making the University of Sydney NTEU branch the trendsetter for the whole sector.

Within a few days, more than 300 members of the union around Australia had signed the *NTEU Fightback* statement along the lines of the University of Sydney censure motion. The statement rejected concessions on wages and conditions and set out an alternative strategy. It demanded firstly that the government fully fund the sector to secure the future of the entire workforce, including casuals, and secondly that

19. NTEU Fightback – No Concessions Facebook page; NTEU Fightback website.

the union must fight against any attacks on jobs, wages or conditions. As Torlakovic and Kuhn put it in *Red Flag* in April, "There is only one way for NTEU members to draw a line: by voting down any attacks on conditions and ultimately backing that up with an industrial campaign. Such a campaign could reverse the appalling message national NTEU leaders have sent to university bosses and the government – that we are a pushover".[20]

In response to the spectre of collaboration and concessions, thousands of members engaged with the union in unprecedented ways. Overwhelming majorities at mass branch meetings at Sydney, RMIT and La Trobe universities passed motions against concessions, despite officials attempting to undemocratically squash them. At Sydney University, a second mass meeting was called and a large majority of the 250 members who attended reaffirmed their opposition. At La Trobe, which does not have a reputation as a highly engaged, independent branch, the leadership attempted to stop a vote being held. Undeterred, the members held a second meeting the following day in which the "no concessions" motion was passed 71 to five. Significant opposition to the union leaders' proposals was quickly registered at members' meetings at Monash University, Flinders University and UNSW. Casuals' networks and some branch committees also passed motions of opposition in the first few weeks.[21]

The revolt against union officials' attempts to stifle debate further galvanised new activists. At RMIT University, the branch experienced a Spartacus moment. A meeting on 15 May maxed out its Zoom capacity of 400, its largest ever branch meeting. After a lengthy defence of the union's strategy from an official and a much shorter rebuttal by NTEU Fightback activist and Socialist Alternative member Liam Ward, union officials tried to stop a vote. Sick of being talked at, and sick of being ignored by the officials, members suddenly began to unmute themselves to vote, declaring "I support Liam" one after the other. Hundreds of individual members voting in this way decided the matter and sent a clear message to the union leaders present.[22]

After a month of closed-door negotiations, union members were finally informed of the deal's substance in mid-April, with full details not available until mid-May. The framework would allow university bosses to impose pay cuts of up to 15 percent. When the officials refused to accept that this figure was accurate, NTEU Fightback's daily emails and Facebook posts provided the proof, right down to the arithmetic. For someone on the median female wage of $65,000, the NTEU officials' deal would mean a pay cut of up to $375 a fortnight. These cuts would have been – and still will be where the zombie framework is implemented at a local level – the biggest wage cut in the sector in living memory. For tens of thousands of workers struggling to survive in a new global depression, these cuts would be life-changing. Many university bosses cynically distanced themselves from this staggering figure, appearing magnanimous by simply asking staff not to take scheduled pay rises. This is a disastrous position for the union to have put itself in.

For activists in the NTEU Fightback group, as well as providing the facts of the officials' sell-out deal, this was a tremendous opportunity to play a role in every area of organis-ing. The solid majorities against the framework at the union's largest branches, Sydney, RMIT and Melbourne, came about because of the detailed groundwork undertaken by Social-ist Alternative members and others in the NTEU Fightback campaign. Local area meetings, many in faculties and divisions that had not held union meetings in decades, allowed rank and file members to analyse the framework and hear the NTEU Fightback critique, and discuss an alternative strategy based

22. Wood and Torlakovic 2020.

on class struggle. Where Socialist Alternative does not have a presence, our activists backed the efforts of others to organise, zooming into member meetings, advising militants, writing documents for their benefit. Ultimately 1,300 union members signed up to campaign for a No vote against the proposed deal. These activists received a regular bulletin from NTEU Fightback, filled with arguments, anecdotes and facts needed to win the debate at a grassroots level.

In response to this unprecedented opposition from members, the NTEU leadership resorted to undemocratic measures. At meetings around the country, members were prevented from putting motions or amendments, calling for debate or even speaking. The chat function in Zoom was often disabled and all sorts of bureaucratic arguments were used to stop members from exercising what should be a basic right for a union member – talking about and voting on industrial strategy in their branch.

A hastily called "meeting of national councillors" rammed through a vote backing the national executive's strategy of collaborating with management by a vote of 89 to 13. This was then touted as a vote of confidence in the strategy. As Socialist Alternative member of NTEU national council Katie Wood wrote:

> Before the vote, about which we had only just been informed, we were shown a professionally produced video that announced, "national councillors have voted". The mover of the leadership's motion proclaimed this the most important decision in the history of the union – yet the meeting of 100-odd was given 20 minutes to debate it.[23]

The national leadership also instructed its paid staff to block the distribution of vote No material and told branch presidents to clamp down on dissent. The national executive used the circular argument that the framework was official union policy

---

23. Wood 2020a.

because they and two meetings of national councillors had already voted for it. Yet at that point members had yet to even have the chance to vote on the JPF in a membership ballot. These tactics fuelled anger among members, but also confidence, knowing that the leadership could not win the argument in a fair and open contest.[24]

Union members at the University of New England (UNE) were among the first to campaign to vote No to the framework, having had very recent experience of the national executive pushing through a deal with management which contradicted members' interests and their express wishes, in their last enterprise agreement negotiations. As Tim Battin, a member of the union branch committee at UNE, explained:

> The NTEU national and state officers wore the members down by spooking them about UNE management's supposed intention to terminate the agreement. It should be said that at no stage did management ever use those words to us, the local reps. Once the deal was made, the NTEU state and national officers sent "vote yes" emails that looked like they came from the branch. The branch had to rely on sending its own emails to urge members to vote no. The branch organiser was told not to send emails that contradicted the national and state position.[25]

The framework was withdrawn on 26 May. This was a vindication of all the rank and file NTEU activists across the country who organised themselves in their workplaces to oppose it. Branch after branch had rejected the framework. Even on the day of its demise, meetings of hundreds at the Australian National University and Monash University passed motions of opposition.

But none of that was automatic, indeed it was unprecedented. The work of the NTEU Fightback campaign, and of the Socialist Alternative members within it, was essential in

24. Wood and Torlakovic 2020.
25. Battin and Macaulay 2020.

achieving this result. Pushing ahead with the vital work of contacting union members across the country, winning the arguments to oppose the officials' sell-out, finding the next person who could be convinced to stand up at a union meeting and argue against the framework, endless debates, arranging meetings on campus after campus, were the essential rank and file organising without which opposition to the framework would have remained isolated, a source of discontent amongst like-minded friends.

Instead, the campaign against the framework energised an activist minority of members of the union in an unprecedented way. That puts union activists in a position to resist the further attacks on jobs or conditions already on their way. And it raises a different idea of what a union should be – one that stands up for its members and refuses to accept that workers should bear the cost of this historic crisis. The campaign to vote No was not just some exercise in "getting the vote out" as some sectarian naysayers have argued. Convincing members to vote No required an activist orientation to build strength on the ground. Unfortunately, the potential of this kind of momentum is still being ignored by the official structures of the union as they pursue the concessional bargaining of the national framework at a local level.[26]

Socialists in the NTEU

The fight within the NTEU posed the question of how socialists should respond to a union sell-out in a very concrete way. It was not enough to mouth support for the idea of rank and file activity: individual socialist activists and members of socialist organisations had to put forward serious arguments for how to develop an independent approach to the NTEU national leadership. Unfortunately most of the socialist left in the NTEU failed to do this, which meant they had no principled answer to the officials' sell-out.

26. Wood and Torlakovic 2020.

The worst were those socialists who had become part of the leadership of the NTEU itself. They included Damien Cahill, assistant secretary of the New South Wales Division, NSW state secretary Michael Thomson, and Alison Barnes, the NTEU national president. Compared to other NTEU officials, their personal histories and writings seem to mark them out as leftists but their practice today is very different.

In his youth Cahill was the editor of the University of Wollongong student newspaper and used the paper to promote a revival of student protest and activism. As an academic Cahill has spent years writing and researching neoliberalism: his staff biography on the University of Sydney website states that he "is particularly interested in the relationship between neoliberal theory and practice, reasons for the durability of neoliberalism, and the ways it is being re-shaped by crisis". However, faced by the implementation of neoliberalism in the universities, Cahill only waved it through in the form of the JPF.

Thomson is a former member and close collaborator of the socialist group Solidarity. In recent years he has worked with the NTEU national leadership to stifle rank and file activity. Just last year he was a key player in the disgraceful betrayal of staff at the University of New England, where he helped impose a nationally negotiated enterprise agreement in the teeth of opposition from rank and file members and the elected branch committee.[27]

Barnes was in the 1990s a member of the International Socialist Organisation. Today, she has been campaigning across the country and throughout the national media for the framework deal with the university bosses, of which she was the key architect. Any left credentials Barnes might have were put to use to more effectively sell the deal, which she charac-terised as an intervention by the union "to put income security and fairness at the centre of a national response" to COVID-19.[28]

27. Battin and Macaulay 2020.
28. Quoted in Marin-Guzman 2020.

No mention in any of her public pronouncements that the deal included wage cuts of up to 15 percent.

As this indicates, the response of these leftists to the current university crisis was indistinguishable from the rest of the union leadership. They have all argued that making concessions to the VCs is the only way to get them to agree to reduce the number of planned redundancies. The idea of fighting them was never mentioned. Instead, the seat at the negotiating table is everything. As Alison Barnes wrote on the NTEU website on 20 May: "But the kicker in the framework is that staff play a central role in crafting and implementing it".[29]

The role of socialists in this situation had to be to help lead and organise the rank and file to stand on their own feet and defend themselves. When union officials work with bosses to attack their own members, it should be straightforward for socialists that you have to take on the officials, too. From 8 April *Red Flag* argued that:

> [T]o really protect job security in universities, we need: Government funding and use of universities' reserves and credit facilities to sustain jobs, and the quality of education, with no strings attached. Full transparency about negotiations between NTEU officials, bosses and the government. Mass online meetings, with scope for debate, to assess the progress of negotiations and to vote on any proposed national agreement. A national campaign, including the possibility of industrial action around our demands on government and university managements.[30]

This strategy was met with significant opposition from the two other organised socialist groups in the NTEU, Socialist Alliance and Solidarity. Throughout the course of the campaign it became obvious that Socialist Alliance and Solidarity had developed substantially different and counterposed strategies for union work to those argued for by Socialist Alternative.

29. Barnes 2020.
30. Torlakovic and Kuhn 2020a.

Instead of trying to cohere, deepen and lead the rank-and-file anger to the NTEU leadership, Socialist Alliance and Solidarity gave the NTEU bureaucrats left cover. That is, at a time when absolute clarity was needed on the lines of division within the union – between those campaigning to push through a wage-cutting deal and those opposing it – they constantly blurred that divide, taking the heat off the officials.

So, for example, Socialist Alliance, whose members include the presidents of the James Cook University and Charles Sturt University NTEU branches, fudged these lines of division in their first *Green Left Weekly (GLW)* article about the fight within the NTEU. As debate raged in the union, *GLW* published an article on 21 April entitled "University unionists call for unity in debate over directions". Members at Sydney University had already rejected the idea of trading off wages and conditions by 117 to 2, and three branches of the union had already passed motions censuring the national executive. The moment required that the left strongly back those organising opposition to the officials' sell-out. *GLW* however simply argued lamely: "NTEU members differ on how best to fight in this situation. They are united in wanting to campaign to win public emergency and long-term higher education funding and opposition to unilateral cuts by management".[31]

Very briefly, in mid-May, more than a month after the campaign kicked off, *GLW* struck a more oppositional tone, publishing two articles attacking the deal and calling for a No vote. But this approach was short-lived. On 28 May, once the framework was defeated, *GLW* returned to its earlier position, trying to give the best possible gloss to the leaders who had tried to foist wage cuts on the membership, quoting Barnes' claim that "The NTEU will now escalate to what will be historically high levels of industrial disputation".[32] This statement was

31. Strauss 2020.
32. Price 2020.

nothing but hot air, a manoeuvre by the officials who, recognising the blow to their credibility with activist members of the union as a result of their support for the JPF, tried to turn on some militant rhetoric. *GLW*, however, simply published the statement as good coin.

Solidarity, a small socialist group primarily based in Sydney, also weakened the campaign through their destructive intervention. While Solidarity members do not currently occupy full-time official positions within the union, the group has worked closely with Thomson for many years, producing a serious softness within their organisation towards him and other NTEU officials.

Very early in the campaign it became clear that the question of voting No to pay cuts and reduced conditions was central to building a fightback. The left officials were quite prepared to denounce the Morrison government's refusal to fund higher education properly, as they were the vice-chancellors' announcements of redundancies. The officials explained at great length the damage that years of bipartisan neoliberal policies had done to the university sector. But one thing they could not tolerate was the demand that members vote No to their wage-cutting deal.

Solidarity only helped to muddy the waters in this respect. At organising meetings, they were for anything but exposing the clearly counterposed positions of the rank and file militants and the left-talking officials. In the name of "unity" with the officials trying to cut members' wages, their members refused to make "vote No" the central demand of the campaign. At a National Higher Education Action Network meeting on 8 May, UTS staff member Paddy Gibson, a member of Solidarity, baldly stated "I'm not going to hand out leaflets outside UTS saying vote against our national officials". Solidarity members tried to caricature the "vote No" campaign by saying that that its proponents had no plans for anything else, that it was a diversion, or that the ballot was only a rumour. This was mere cover for their refusal to condemn the leadership, which they are personally and politically close to.

This approach has continued. More recently at UTS Solidarity members opposed a motion calling for "no concessions", instead supporting a motion from the branch officials that both sets the framework for concessional bargaining, and enables management to force workers to take accumulated leave. This prelude to mass sackings was described as "an incredibly minor agreement variation".[33]

In place of a solid "vote No" campaign against the framework, Solidarity preferred to prioritise a National Day of Action (NDA) that had the support of the same officials pushing the JPF. Wherever they existed Solidarity argued that this stunt – rather than the vote No campaign – should be the focus for NTEU activists. Their main concern was to win the union leadership's endorsement of the NDA, and so they were initially opposed to including "vote No" materials and slogans for the day. They boasted of their private overtures to the left officials, that they were winning them over to the idea. But they were pushing at an open door. The national executive grasped the NDA with both hands since they understood that it would be a great opportunity to give themselves the appearance of fighting the cuts while at the same time implementing them. They put on a big promotion campaign for the NDA, proclaiming the day as "Epic!" In reality, the NDA passed most members by, but the left officials threw themselves into it. Cahill and Thomson took a break from ramming through a 15 percent wage cut to join the car convoy in Sydney, while Barnes took part in a national livestream alongside university managers in which she argued for the framework to an audience of hundreds.

Under pressure from the rank-and-file rebellion and left-wing criticism, Solidarity modified their approach late in the campaign, acting as if they had never argued against a "vote No" campaign. Yet as late as 23 May at a Sydney University

---

33. Rose 2020.

staff and student meeting, they were still complaining in the Zoom chat that demanding the campaign be centred on voting No to the sell-out deal was "disrupting the ability of rank and file activists and union officials to work together".

For many years the retreat of the union movement and the small size of the socialist left meant socialists had few opportunities to lead rank and file work. As union milieus shrank, sections of the socialist left have become increasingly close to left-talking union officials, who tend to be happy to sign endorsement letters and speak at rallies rather than defending their members' interests. While some of this collaboration is of course necessary, many on the left have gradually adjusted their approach to the bureaucracy, accommodating to their conservatism. The rank and file revolt in the NTEU exposes this long term tendency, and marks a qualitative break in the behaviour of the socialists groups mentioned above.

Arguing for unionists to resist all forms of class collaboration and understanding the role of trade union officials who promote it are key issues for the left. These arguments echo an older debate among socialists. Historically, many socialists have veered between two wrong positions. A small number have simply written off the left officials and refused to work with them and the unions more broadly on principle, because of their record of selling out rank and file members. This is a mistake. Even the most despicable union boss can on occasions lead actions that have the potential to build rank and file power and organisation. Much more common, however, is the approach of just tailing behind them, apologising for and covering up their betrayals. The rationale for this approach is that by developing close relationships with individuals in positions of influence – and perhaps even taking those positions themselves – socialists can impact the broader class struggle more effectively. Yet maintaining a permanent alliance with reformist officials – particularly in the current era – requires unconscionable compromises. Partly this is because there are no left officials in the way that the distinction was once understood, but even in the glory days of unionism the left officials always proved to be ultimately more loyal to the rest of the union machinery and the employers than to the workers. The best approach was summarised by union delegates in Scotland's industrial heartlands back in 1915: "We will support the officials just so long as they rightly represent the workers, but we will act independently immediately if they misrepresent them".[34]

Why has the socialist left in Australia developed very different strategies? This question can't be disentangled from the broader context in which the left has had to operate over the last couple of decades. It has been a difficult period. The workers' movement has been in retreat and, outside of occasional outbursts, street protests and social movements have also been limited. The scope for socialists to connect their ideas of working-class self-activity and militancy to sections of organised workers has been extremely limited, a situation reinforced by the small size of the socialist left. In related but different ways Socialist Alliance and Solidarity have adapted to a significant degree to this period of working-class weakness. For the Alliance this has been most clear in regard to the watering down of their politics into electoral work that has at any rate produced few gains, and their adaptations to various fads on the international left: broad parties, identity politics, reformism and so on.[35] For Solidarity it has been expressed by their conservative attitude to the Labor Party and the Greens and their conservative approach to work in the refugee movement. Most spectacularly, Solidarity have recently opposed calls to stop Adani or for an immediate end to fossil fuels, insisting that these left-wing slogans undermine the potential for union action around climate change.[36]

---

34. Hinton 1973, p296.
35. See the debate in the *Marxist Left Review* between Socialist Alternative and the Socialist Alliance: Oakley 2013, Fredman, Hinman and Price 2013.
36. See Solidarity 2020 for their position and Hassan 2020 for a critique of Solidarity's right-wing approach.

In the NTEU, both groups have developed cosy relationships towards left-sounding trade union officials for a variety of reasons. In a flat political and industrial climate, it often appeared as if the only work you could do within the union movement were campaigns in collaboration with union officialdom. This is an objectively difficult situation, however the Alliance and Solidarity approach has simply built illusions in the union bureaucracy. One example of this has been their trumpeting of union officials that have been willing to pass motions or speak at rallies around refugee rights, the environment and LGBTI issues. The mistake isn't in asking them to do this, or in passing motions in union meetings on broader political issues. The issue is not being clear on how such activities provide cover for officials, giving the impression that they are more radical than they really are. The *International Socialism* journal commented on this phenomenon in the context of the Campaign for Nuclear Disarmament in the 1960s: "Sometimes it is their very distance from their members, their very middle-classness, that makes union officials the more receptive to CND propaganda".[37]

Instead of trying to create whatever independent space within the unions that is possible, Solidarity and Socialist Alliance have developed a symbiotic relationship with sections of the left trade union bureaucracy. Often this was justified by reference to the divisions between right-wing and left-wing officials, and repetition of the argument that socialists should exploit those divisions to advance working-class struggle. But that was not the question at issue here. The issue confronting union members was officials who claim to be the left acting just as reprehensibly as some of the right-wing unions. As Gluckstein and Cliff put it in their extensive study of socialists and trade union work:

A revolutionary party must know how to exploit the division

---

between left and right bureaucrats, between those who are prepared to make militant speeches (even if they will not act upon them) and those who are openly wedded to conciliation at all times. Through using this division the independence, initiative and self-confidence of the rank and file may be strengthened, on one condition: the party must make clear that the rank and file cannot trust the left officials or put their faith in radical rhetoric... An alliance with left bureaucrats is only a means to broad action... Such an alliance, like every other tactic in the trade union field, must be judged by one criterion, and one criterion only – whether it raises the activity, and hence the confidence and consciousness of the workers.[38]

As we have seen with regard to the NTEU Fightback campaign, the Alliance and Solidarity did not use divisions within the NTEU officials to help build rank and file activity. To the contrary, it was the union officialdom who exploited sections of the socialist left in order to blur the key division in the union between those who wanted to fight, and those who advocated surrender ahead of the battle.

In practice what the Alliance and Solidarity have done is resurrect the old reformist approach to union officialdom that was pursued by Social Democratic and Communist parties for many decades. While they too mouthed support for the idea of rank and file activity they confined their actual intervention to creating left-wing pressure groups on the bureaucracy. These groups were formally separate to the official leadership but politically and strategically subservient to them. Like the Alliance and Solidarity today they constantly pushed the line that united action means downplaying the differences between the union bureaucracy and the rank and file. Solidarity's criticism that Socialist Alternative's approach to the NTEU

---

38. Cliff and Gluckstein 1986. It is worth noting that Solidarity is the official International Socialist Tendency group in Australia and comes from the same political tradition as Tony Cliff and Donny Gluckstein. This makes the conservative nature of their intervention into the NTEU Fightback campaign all the more remarkable.

undermined the possibility of united action sounds very similar to former Communist Party of Australia leader Bernie Taft's criticism that the radical NSW Builders Labourers' Federation had "a tendency to counterpose the rank-and-file movement to the trade union officials".[39]

All of this raises the question of what a rank-and-file strategy actually means. Today most socialists claim to agree with a rank and file approach to trade union work, interpreted narrowly as a focus on "workplace mapping" paired with some on the ground organising. Grassroots organising is of course the basis of good unionism, however it is not in and of itself a rank and file strategy. Trade union officials can engage in on the ground organising if they want to break into a new industry or wish to shore up their current membership. Even right-wing organisations such as the Catholic-dominated Industrial Groups of the 1950s used grassroots organising in the unions in order to fight against the influence of the Communist Party and the left. A rank and file strategy is one that builds on democratic grassroots organising combined with a political and strategic independence from union officialdom and their pro-capitalist ideologies. This means fighting to deepen the understanding of rank and file activists that the strategies of union officials will end in defeat, that they have different interests from the mass of ordinary workers, that it is through industrial struggle that workers have their greatest strength, and that it is in the interests of rank and file workers to fight around broader political issues.

In our own modest way this is what Socialist Alternative has tried to do wherever we can. We face, of course, the same difficult objective conditions referenced earlier. But instead of sucking up to union officials and other reformist institutions as a shortcut to mass influence, we have pursued a more modest, but more politically serious response. For example,

---

39. See Mick Armstrong, "The NSW BLF: The battle to tame the concrete jungle" elsewhere in this issue..

when COVID-19 hit, members of Socialist Alternative organised a campaign within English-language schools that defeated managements' attempts to impose a 15 percent pay cut.[40] In 2016 members of Socialist Alternative working at the Polar Fresh warehouse played a leading role in a significant three-day strike involving hundreds of workers.[41] You could add to this dozens more examples of smaller workplace-based actions organised or supported by our members. Much of this activity has been modest in scale and none of it is anywhere near enough to turn the tide in the class struggle, but the experience means we can be confident that an alternative strategy to class collaboration and concession bargaining is viable. We have been prepared to work with trade union officials on joint campaigns where possible, for instance with the National Union of Workers during the pickets at the Baiada chicken factory in 2011 and at the Chemist Warehouse strikes last year, while aware of the difficulties in maintaining independent and critical assessments of their approach to the fights at hand.

As a national rank-and-file rebellion, NTEU Fightback was on a very different scale to anything previously attempted. It was only made possible because we had built up an organisation of over 400 socialist activists over the last two decades, primarily but not exclusively recruited from the university campuses.

The rebuilding of a serious rank-and-file current is then bound up in the broader reconstruction of a revolutionary socialist left in Australia. Historically the revivals in rank-and-file trade union activity have always been intertwined with broader radicalisation and the expansion of the socialist left. As we enter into a period of greater political and economic turmoil in the wake of COVID-19, strengthening the forces of revolutionary socialism is vital to rebuilding the possibilities of rank-and-file militant action. This is all the more important

---

40. An IH teacher 2020.
41. Small 2016.

when union officialdom is so acquiescent in the face of attacks from bosses and the government.

Analysing the conflicting arguments and positions of different groups of socialists towards union officials in the NTEU is not, therefore, an arcane theoretical or sectarian exercise. Sectarianism is about putting the organisation ahead of the movement, but in this case there would have been no movement whatsoever had the approach of the rest of the left been adopted. As in so many cases, it was the revolutionary politics of the comrades at the heart of NTEU Fightback that made the movement possible to begin with, and seeking clarity on these questions is in the interests of all involved.

Future challenges

While the JPF was defeated at a national level, the sector remains mired in a profound and long-term crisis. The argument for concession bargaining therefore has not and will not recede. While the national organising against the framework allowed a militant minority to put political pressure on union leaders, the balance of forces is far less favourable at a local level.

At the only three campuses where VCs signed up to the framework – UWA, La Trobe and Monash – the NTEU leadership have continued to push ahead with their deal. They have won votes to do so on all three campuses, resulting in big wage cuts, compulsory taking of annual leave and the gutting of major change clauses in enterprise agreements, which gives the green light to further attacks.[42] Unfortunately the active and more left-wing minority who had been voting solidly against the framework in numerous meetings did not have the time and capacity to convince the broader majority on these campuses. But even where universities have not signed up to the JPF, the union's announcement in April of their pre-emptive surrender has given vice-chancellors the go-ahead to implement savage

42. Fieldes 2020; NTEU Fightback 2020.

attacks, in particular against those whose employment was already precarious. Universities everywhere have sacked casual staff in their thousands, and refused to extend fixed-term contracts. La Trobe University vice-chancellor John Dewar boasted that $7 million had been saved at his institution by cutting casual jobs.[43]

Bosses at Melbourne University, one of the wealthiest institutions in Australia, were the first outside the three JPF campuses to try to exploit the weakness shown by the NTEU officials' offer of concessions, demanding to take back a 2.2 percent pay rise from their employees and worsen redundancy conditions. They were defeated by an incredible burst of worker organising. Over ten days, more than 1,700 workers attended 18 meetings in their local work areas to discuss management's attack and the union's response. As Katie Wood, who played a leading role in this, wrote:

> Management at one of the wealthiest and most powerful institutions in the country was defeated by systematic worker organisation. This kind of organising drive has no parallel in recent years either at Melbourne University or in higher education more broadly. It's a welcome shift from the dominant approach of unions in Australia, and the national leadership of the NTEU in particular, who have expressed a deep pessimism about the ability to organise workers in the workplace in order to resist – and used that pessimistic outlook as a justification for signing terrible, wage-cutting deals with management at many campuses. The fantastic burst of organising at the University of Melbourne is exactly the antidote required. One example among many: in Veterinary and Agricultural Sciences, 45 people attended the first union meeting in living memory in the faculty, with 76 Zooming in for a second meeting before the vote.

Of 8,069 staff who voted, 5,190 – an incredible 64 percent – voted No.[44]

---

43. Vassiley and Broadbent 2020.
44. Wood 2020b.

This massive victory, underpinned by a surge in grassroots organising, was kicked off with minimal support from the state or national offices of the union. It speaks volumes about the priorities of the union office that more resources were being put into selling a union-negotiated variation of the national framework at La Trobe than into resisting an employer-sponsored attack at Melbourne. The only serious intervention of the national leadership into the early part of the campaign was an email from the national secretary to all members, which chose to re-prosecute the arguments for the wage-cutting national framework and the importance of a Yes vote at La Trobe! Additional resources were eventually allocated for the last few days of phone-banking, but the victory belongs to the branch delegates and activists, not to the architects of the framework.[45]

This was an extremely significant result. It sent a message to higher education workers everywhere that it was possible to defeat employer-sponsored attacks on wages and conditions and encouraged them to continue to resist. But so far it has been an isolated success for rank and file organising. Western Sydney University and the University of Tasmania have seen union-management schemes which reduce staff pay voted into being.[46] Everywhere the union machine continues to push concessions rather than oppose them. Even in her (very muted) response to the Melbourne Uni victory, NTEU national president Alison Barnes sought to foist the framework back on the Melbourne University branch, pleading with management: "We have negotiated a framework which allows for temporary pay reductions to save jobs, provided vice chancellors are transparent about their finances and open to co-operative negotiation".[47] Rather than taking the victory at Melbourne Uni as an indication that workers can fight off concessions through

45. Wood 2020b.
46. NTEU Fightback 2020.
47. Evans 2020.

a rank and file organising effort, the national officials took it as an opportunity to advertise their openness to concessions so long as they are involved in negotiating them. Worst of all, the non-union ballot was offering only to withdraw the 2.2 percent wage rise, rather than offering a 15 percent pay cut – workers were objectively better off with a non-union ballot than a union one!

The situation remains a difficult one. As NTEU Fightback argued from the outset, the framework did nothing to save jobs. Already among the campuses that endorsed it, Monash is slashing 277 jobs and La Trobe, despite staff voting to support a 10 percent wage cut under the framework, has announced there will be between 215 and 415 redundancies. The NTEU's offer of the framework at UNSW merely emboldened management to unilaterally announce 493 redundancies. While the stunning success of the rank and file organising effort at Melbourne University has not been replicated elsewhere, there are other campuses like the University of Wollongong where the union managed to defeat a management-initiated ballot. The downside to 62 percent opposing the employer's attack is that the officials immediately reiterated their only objection to concessions – that they want to be involved in devising them. In mid-July their wish came true: 84 percent of union members voted in favour of an NTEU-brokered wage cut via the deferral of two pay rises until 2022, no pay rises upon promotion, and agreement to undertake different work at management's direction. All this for the most tepid management commitment of all the miserable unenforceable promises to date: "no forced redundancies directly due to COVID-19" before 20 April 2021.[48] As the combined efforts of the NTEU machine and ACTU call centre resources to get a Yes vote to wage cuts and other concessions at the three framework campuses showed, there are forces other than the bosses arrayed against the rank and file. The forces of resistance are

48. Campus Morning Mail 2020.

small and scattered, so we have an uphill battle ahead; but the NTEU Fightback slogan "Vote No and keep organising" is the only way forward.

Conclusion

The argument that workers' interests can best be protected by collaborating with bosses will not be confined to the NTEU. Clarifying the approach socialists should take to union officials is absolutely necessary if we are going to build the fightback we need. Capitalism is now in a long-term, structural crisis, which will result in wave after wave of attacks on workers in every sector. Organising to rebuild a class-struggle current in our unions has never been more urgent.

In fighting attempts to gut their jobs, pay and conditions, university workers are doing more than standing up for their individual rights. They can begin to provide a lead to the broader union movement, making an argument that can inspire others to refuse to make sacrifices for the sake of bosses' profit margins. Some supporters of the NTEU officials have made the all too familiar argument that university workers must sacrifice to avoid alienating workers who don't have the conditions they enjoy. But what of the tens of thousands of families and dependents who rely on the incomes of university workers, many of them on already low wages? Far from alienating other workers, a serious campaign to defend NTEU members' existing wages and conditions can show others how to fight for their own.

Unfortunately, workers have to be prepared to wage this fight against not just the bosses and the government, but our union leaders too. Yet there are many allies who would be ready to assist if called upon. Students in Australia and around the world have proven to be key allies of university staff. The successful student-staff campaign to defeat university deregulation under former prime minister Tony Abbott showed that this alliance can cause a crisis for elites and win support from the wider public. If matched with widespread industrial action, who knows what could be won. Building a network of grassroots militants around NTEU Fightback – and the Socialist Alternative caucus that is at its core – is the necessary first step in that direction.

References

An IH teacher 2020, "English teachers defeat bosses' attacks in pandemic", *Red Flag*, 9 April. https://redflag.org.au/node/7121.

Barnes, Alison 2020, "Job-saving deal will give university workforce a say in their future", NTEU website, 20 May. https://www.nteu.org.au/article/Job-saving-deal-will-give-university-workforce-a-say-in-their-future-22060.

Barrigos, Rebecca 2013, "The neoliberal transformation of higher education", *Marxist Left Review*, 6, Winter. https://marxistleftreview.org/articles/the-neoliberal-transformation-of-higher-education/.

Battin, Tim and Alex Macaulay 2020, "How the NTEU's national leadership made a bad deal at UNE", *Red Flag*, 18 May. https://redflag.org.au/node/7189 .

Bramble, Tom 2018, "Our unions in crisis: How did it come to this?", *Marxist Left Review*, 15, Summer. https://marxistleftreview.org/articles/our-unions-in-crisis-how-did-it-come-to-this/.

Campus Morning Mail, "Worked-out in Wollongong", 17 July. https://campusmorningmail.com.au/news/worked-out-in-wollongong/.

Cliff, Tony and Donny Gluckstein 1986, *Marxism and Trade Union Struggle – The General Strike of 1926*, chapter 2. https://www.marxists.org/archive/cliff/works/1986/tradeunion/ch02.htm#d18.

Duffy, Connor 2020, "Government announces coronavirus relief package for higher education with focus on domestic students", ABC, 12 April. https://www.abc.net.au/news/2020-04-12/government-announces-coronavirus-higher-education-relief-package/12142752.

Evans, Michael 2020, "Media Release: Uni of Melbourne staff reject unfair offer", NTEU, 11 June. https://www.nteu.org.au/article/Media-Release%3A-Uni-of-Melbourne-staff-reject-unfair-offer-22111.

Ferguson, Hazel and Henry Sherrell 2019, "Overseas students in Australian higher education: a quick guide", 20 June. https://www.aph.gov.au/About_Parliament/Parliamentary_Departments/Parliamentary_Library/pubs/rp/rp1819/Quick_Guides/OverseasStudents.

Fieldes, Diane 2020, "The university pay cut deal is defeated. It's a win for rank and file activism", *Red Flag*, 26 May. https://redflag.org.au/node/7199.

Fredman, Nick, Pip Hinman and Susan Price 2013, "Revolutionary unity to meet the capitalist crisis", *Marxist Left Review*, 6, Winter. https://marxistleftreview.org/articles/revolutionary-unity-to-meet-the-capitalist-crisis/.

Hassan, Omar 2020, "No excuses – we have to shut down the fossil fuel industry", *Red Flag*, 14 February. https://redflag.org.au/node/7022.

Hinton, James 1973, *The First Shop Stewards' Movement*, George Allen and Unwin.

Hurley, Peter 2020, "Australian universities could lose $19 billion in the next 3 years. Our economy will suffer with them", *The Conversation*, 17 April. https://theconversation.com/australian-universities-could-lose-19-billion-in-the-next-3-years-our-economy-will-suffer-with-them-136251.

International Socialism 1960, "Editorial: A Blow Against the Boss is a Blow Against the Bomb", *International Socialism*, 2, Autumn. https://www.marxists.org/history/etol/newspape/isj/1960/isj002/editorial1.htm.

Kuhn, Rick and Jack Hynes 2020, "Why the university workers' fight matters", *Red Flag*, 8 May. https://redflag.org.au/node/7170.

Long, Colin 2018, "Casualisation of university workforce is a national disgrace", *Sydney Morning Herald*, 3 August. https://www.smh.com.au/education/casualisation-of-university-workforce-is-a-national-disgrace-20180803-p4zvcm.html.

Marin-Guzman, David 2020, "Unions at war over deal to cut pay at universities", *Australian Financial Review*, 13 May. https://www.afr.com/work-and-careers/workplace/union-blue-over-nteu-deal-to-cut-pay-at-universities-20200513-p54sfz.

McManus, Sally 2020, on ABC *Insiders*, 5 April. https://www.abc.net.au/insiders/sally-mcmanus-joins-insiders/12123084.

Morrison, Scott 2020, press conference, 2 April. https://www.pm.gov.au/media/press-conference-australian-parliament-house-act-020420.

NTEU Fightback – No Concessions Facebook page 2020. https://www. facebook.com/NTEUfightback.

NTEU Fightback 2020, http://nteufightback.site/.

O'Brien, John 2015, *National Tertiary Education Union. A most unlikely union* (UNSW Press).

O'Shea, Louise 2020, "Beware union leaders bearing deals", *Red Flag*, 10 June. https://redflag.org.au/node/7224.

Oakley, Corey 2013, "What kind of organisation do socialists need?", *Marxist Left Review*, 6, Summer, https://marxistleftreview.org/articles/ what-kind-of-organisation-do-socialists-need/.

Price, Susan 2020, "After debate, NTEU commits to an industrial fight for jobs", *Green Left Weekly*, 28 May. https://www.greenleft.org.au/content/ after-debate-nteu-commits-industrial-fight-jobs.

Rose, Cat 2020, "Fight continues at UTS – despite union leadership", *Red Flag*, 19 July. https://redflag.org.au/node/7269.

Ross, John 2020, "Cut pay for the greater good, Australian academics asked", *Times Higher Education*, 17 April. https://www.timeshighereducation. com/news/cut-pay-greater-good-australian-academics-asked.

Small, Jerome 2016, "'Thirty bucks, no trucks!' Warehouse workers strike back against Coles", *Red Flag*, 31 July. https://redflag.org.au/node/5410.

Solidarity 2020, "Editorial: Election shock – but Morrison can be fought," *Solidarity*, 27 May, https://www.solidarity.net.au/mag/back/2019/126/ editorial-election-shock-but-morrison-can-be-fought/.

Strauss, Jonathan 2020, "University unionists call for unity in debate over directions", *Green Left Weekly*, 21 April. https://www.greenleft.org.au/ content/university-unionists-call-unity-debate-over-directions.

Taylor, Daniel 2020, "'Returning to normal' means launching new attacks", *Red Flag*, 12 May. https://redflag.org.au/node/7178.

Tehan, Dan 2020, press conference, 12 April. https://ministers.dese.gov. au/tehan/minister-education-dan-tehan-and-chief-medical-officer- professor-brendan-murphy-press.

Torlakovic, Alma and Rick Kuhn 2020a, "University workers must not accept wage cuts in exchange for 'job security'", *Red Flag*, 8 April. https:// redflag.org.au/node/7119.

Torlakovic, Alma and Rick Kuhn 2020b, "University workers prepare to fight union over concessions", *Red Flag*, 13 April. https://redflag.org.au/node/7128.

Vassiley, Alexis and Kaye Broadbent 2020, "Universities are cutting hundreds of jobs – they, and the government, can do better", *The Conversation*, 16 July. https://theconversation.com/universities-are-cutting-hundreds-of-jobs-they-and-the-government-can-do-better-142824.

Wood, Katie and Alma Torlakovic 2020, "The rank and file uprising in Australia's higher education union", *Red Flag*, 26 May. https://redflag.org.au/node/7198.

Wood, Katie 2020a, "University workers revolt against union concession plan", *Red Flag*, 25 April, https://redflag.org.au/node/7149.

Wood, Katie 2020b, "Worker organising defeats management at Melbourne Uni", *Red Flag*, 11 June. https://redflag.org.au/node/7227.

JANEY STONE

The real iron ladies: Women in the 1984/85 British miners' strike[1]

Janey Stone is a long-term socialist activist who has written extensively about women's liberation and other topics. Her current focus is with the independent radical publisher Interventions.

The Archbishop of Bologna said to me, through an interpreter, "Your Prime Minister's a woman. And she's an Iron Lady." I said, "Tell him that she might be an Iron Lady, but she didn't bank on thousands of Iron Ladies coming up."

–Miner's wife[2]

THE BRITISH MINERS' strike of 1984/5 was the longest mass strike in European history. After 10 years of economic crisis and rightward political movement, at last a major trade union stood up to Margaret Thatcher. There are political lessons to be learnt from this struggle – about the nature of trade union officials and Labourism, about the methods necessary to win such a class struggle. But there are also other lessons, equally political but not always recognised.

Pessimists constantly declare to socialists: "You can't change human nature." But people – men and women – changed during this strike. In their new-found collective strength, they discovered a new confidence in themselves. They became open

1. Janey arrived in the UK in March 1985, just before the end of the strike. She experienced first hand the galvanising effect the strike had, and was particularly enthused by the transformations experienced by the women. This article is a slightly edited version of the original, first published in *Hecate*, Vol. XI, No. 2, 1985. It draws upon contemporary material but Janey's analysis and conclusion still have central relevance for us today.
2. Quoted in Salt and Layzell 1985.

to new ideas and discarded old prejudices. They changed in the way they behaved towards each other; they found new friends and new hopes.

We saw little of the struggle in Australia apart from shock/ horror stories about picket-line violence. But the experience is highly relevant to anyone working for the liberation of women. Women appear to be absent from much labour history, and their participation in struggles often has to be rediscovered.[3] But in the miners' strike, the active and leading role of women in the mining communities was obvious. Without their support, the strike could not have been maintained for so long. It is with the changes in their consciousness that this article is centrally concerned. But their experience can't be separated from the more general lessons of the strike, and this article also aims to show the interactions between the two.

Mining communities, isolated as they are, tend to be traditional in attitudes. Women in Britain's coalfields were beginning to break out, but change was very slow. The strike altered all that, almost overnight:

> To get up in front of complete strangers of varying age groups, varying occupations...and you think "My god. This time last year I was doing the washing up".[4]

Blood, sweat and tears – the Great Strike

On 1 March 1984, the National Coal Board (NCB) threw down a gauntlet to the National Union of Mineworkers (NUM).[5] They closed Cortonwood, a Yorkshire mine which still had several years of coal in it.

3. As an example see Stone 2008, p6, in which I show that a substantial amount of women's activity during the Depression had previously been ignored, and discuss the reasons for this.
4. Quoted in Salt and Layzell 1985.
5. This account simply summarises the events of the strike. For a more detailed account, and for a discussion of the more contentious points – whether there should have been a national ballot, the arguments about mass picketing, the return to work without a settlement – see Callinicos and Simons 1985.

Politically, Thatcher had served the ruling class well. But economically she had failed – real wages rose while the economy was declining. Her offensive against the working-class movement was aimed not at the destruction of the trade unions but, rather, at their Americanisation – the creation of a weaker, more bureaucratic, less political trade union movement, closely policed by the courts. This could only be achieved by taking on, and decisively defeating, a powerful group of workers. The miners were the obvious candidates.

The Tories had carefully planned the battle. Coal stocks were built up and the police force reorganised and trained in strikebreaking. Already the NCB had closed 23 pits in the previous year and destroyed 21,000 jobs. With Cortonwood, the Yorkshire miners knew it was fight now or never, and they reacted swiftly. Flying pickets brought the rest of Yorkshire to a standstill. Kent and the traditionally militant areas of South Wales and Scotland followed. But in Nottinghamshire (Notts), and other areas, a large percentage of miners remained at work. From the beginning the strike was deprived of solidarity and unity.

This need not have happened. Flying pickets from Yorkshire were initially very successful at picketing out the Notts miners, particularly when they were allowed to talk to them to put their case. But they were up against two obstacles. A massive police operation set out to prevent the pickets from gaining access to the working miners. And the police and government's efforts were aided markedly by the Notts area union officials and right-wing national leaders, who denounced pickets, discouraged miners from joining the strike, and joined in the call for a ballot on the strike. In this, they played straight into the Tories' hands.

The sudden liking for ballots on the part of the press and politicians was sheer hypocrisy. Thatcher had not balloted workers at GCHQ communications centre a few months previously when she banned trade unions there. Nor had miners voted on whether pits should be closed down. The bulk of striking miners believed you shouldn't ballot away other people's jobs. They knew the ballot issue was mainly being used to divide them.[6]

Police sealed off the county to keep out picketers, and their tactics were an exercise in mass intimidation. Eight thousand police swamped Notts. They massed on picket lines and patrolled villages. They beat up individuals. In Blidworth they laid siege to the village, smashed their way into the village hall where the soup kitchen was, and terrorised the women and children inside. In short, it was open season on strikers in the Notts coalfields.[7]

Between them, the police and the union officials succeeded in keeping most of Notts working. The centre of the strike now shifted. Mass picketing of economic targets was now necessary to win – in other words, the methods of the successful 1972 miners' strike.

What became known as the Battle of Orgreave was the turning point. The government wanted to prove that picketing could not succeed. For the miners, it was a chance to turn the tide of the strike. Over several days in May and June, the police were "out to maim not to arrest".[8] The photographs and descriptions of the battles show police in full riot gear with horses and dogs, beating up men in shorts, t-shirts and thongs.

The picket failed, mainly because of failure to organise support. The mass picket at Saltley during the 1972 miners' strike succeeded when 20,000 Birmingham engineering workers joined the miners' picket. Yorkshire NUM did not

---

6. For example: "I ventured to raise the question of a national ballot only to be told in no uncertain terms that you can't ballot jobs." Seaburne 1985.
7. "The Chief Constable of Nottinghamshire...denied police officers had used a crowbar to smash the windscreen of a picket's car. It was, he said, a truncheon." (*Financial Times*, March 1984, quoted in Huddle et al 1985.)
8. Huddle et al 1985. The photographs in this book show graphically the nature of the violence at Orgreave.

attempt to build the Orgreave picket by appeals to rank and file in Sheffield engineering factories. They relied instead on manoeuvres at the top, treating ordinary miners like a stage army.

The remainder of the strike can be summarised in two words – solidarity and bureaucracy. The strike had created enormous sympathy and support from rank-and-file workers and others throughout the country. The railway workers of Coalville sealed off their area. Print workers at the *Sun* twice refused to print blatant and hysterical lies about the miners. By three months into the strike, there were support committees in dozens of cities and towns and, by the summer, twinning (direct linking with a pit) was catching on like wildfire. The *Guardian* estimated that as much as £60m was collected, disproving the claim that the miners had no support among other workers.

But most of the support was spontaneous and local and, contrasting with it, there was Trade Union Congress (TUC) inaction and the failure to spread the struggle to other industries. In steel and on the docks there were opportunities to link local issues with the miners and open another front against Thatcher. But officials' reliance on deals and the weakness of workplace organisation led to more setbacks. Despite the TUC's verbal support of the miners in May, they did nothing to prevent coal and oil entering the power stations. This guaranteed the miners' defeat.

Labour Party activists did much of the work of the miners' support groups, and stirring motions were passed through the party conference. But Neil Kinnock, the Labour Party leader, spent most of his time attacking violence on the picket lines and worrying about his electoral image.

By the winter of 1985, scabbing was increasing, and the miners were feeling a growing sense of directionlessness. They had shown great endurance and spirit against constant police violence, mass arrests, lying, media campaigns and lack of money, while at crucial points their officials had given no leadership. But if outright victory was no longer possible, at least a negotiated settlement would have protected victimised miners and local union organisation. Instead, left-wing union leaders led the movement for a return to work without a settlement. The strike ended on 5 March 1985.

The miners were defeated. But things were not the same as before and, while pit closures hadn't been prevented, something else was gained. As one miner's wife said:

> This strike had extraordinary effects. Out of something that is terrible, something very good has grown.[9]

The women organise

This was very much a strike in which press, employers and government could be expected to appeal to the wives to "see reason" and get the men back to work. But that tactic failed, largely due to the unprecedented widespread formation of women's support groups throughout the mining communities – a mass movement, largely spontaneous, that took everyone by surprise.

The initial media attempt to use women to oppose the strike backfired.[10] The miners' wives were very angry when they saw "what the press and the media were saying about the Nottingham wives taking their husbands into work. We saw

9. Quoted in *Striking Back* 1985.
10. There was some concerted women's anti-strike organising later in the strike. In South Wales, a media-orchestrated campaign failed completely. The women from Maerdy "arrived to counter one of their rallies but missed it because it was assembling in a telephone box". The most notorious case was Irene McGibbons, leader of the Miners' Wives Back to Work Movement, and supposedly a simple miner's wife from Kent. Actually, she had been the leader of the infamous "Cowley Wives", who organised a successful victimisation campaign against an elected shop steward in British Leyland in 1974. She stood as a Conservative candidate in a council election in 1983 and owned her own textile business and guesthouse. During the strike, her husband scabbed in Kent. Two weeks after denying any connection with the Tories, she received a standing ovation at their conference. (Sweeney 1985, Hollingsworth 1984.)

absolute red!"[11] This motive also inspired women at Yorkshire Main colliery near Doncaster:

> It started because I couldn't stand TV making out that the wives weren't behind their men. I was so angry and frustrated for a week... [We] decided to go and picket Thorseby in Nottinghamshire that night... We called ourselves an action group because everyone says they support the miners, but we want to be active.
>
> As we walked up to Thorseby the pickets were moaning "Oh god not the women again". They'd had the local wives nagging them, but when they found out we were from Yorkshire this fantastic cheer went up. It was brilliant.[12]

They followed this up by hand-writing leaflets and distributing them through doors. Fifteen women came to a meeting, and they set up a strikers' kitchen.

All over the coalfields, the same thing was happening. Some women wanted to make a public stand. Others wanted simply to do something about the financial and other burdens that the strike imposed on the families. In some cases, the groups were initiated by experienced feminists, trade unionists, Labour Party or Communist Party members, or wives of NUM officials, such as Betty Heathfield. In many other cases, the women had no previous experience at all. Lorraine Johnson, secretary of the Bold group in Lancashire, had experience of public speaking consisting of having called the numbers at the old folks bingo!

> We had to find out for ourselves how to do it... There was no book in the library to tell us what to do![13]

In some cases, the women did have some experience to draw upon. In 1972 in Betteshanger, Kent, women had taken on picketing when the men had to leave to picket power stations.

---

11. Quoted in Salt and Layzell 1985.
12. Quoted in Callinicos and Simons 1985.
13. Quoted in Salt and Layzell 1985.

One woman recalled how a driver was astonished when they arrived at Betteshanger to be confronted by a picket entirely of women.[14] This sort of experience no doubt contributed to the speed with which Betteshanger women organised themselves into a support group two weeks after the strike began.

One significant aspect of the spontaneous movement was the strong desire for autonomy; the women wanted to run things themselves. Everywhere were heard comments like: "This is our group, we started it up and we are going to say how to run it."[15] The women did not of course want to dissociate themselves from the union and the struggle, but they did want organisational control over their activities. This urge for control was not because they felt their interests in any way opposed to those of the male strikers – over and over again, the wives emphasised that the only reason they began to organise was in order to "help the NUM in its fight to save our industry".[16] Rather, the desire for independence was a result of the flowering of self-activity and taking control of their own lives that the struggle produced. It was also partly a consequence of the nature of the strike. The trade union officials discouraged rank-and-file activity, and the women (as did the men) learnt that "to do anything during the strike meant relying on yourself and not on the bureaucracy".[17]

The women's groups were active around three main areas: welfare, in particular strike kitchens; campaign work, particularly fundraising and public rallies; and picketing.

Food and welfare

Without the women's support groups supplying food and welfare on a regular basis, there is no doubt that the strike could not have gone on as long as it did. Early in the strike, the

---

14. Dean 1985.
15. Quoted in Dean 1985, p62.
16. Quoted in Dean 1985, p70.
17. "Learning From the Strike" 1985, p9.

Department of Health and Social Security (DHSS) claimed that families were receiving £15 strike pay and therefore deducted this from the benefit it paid strikers. The NUM was not in fact paying strike pay, and so there was a great deal of financial hardship, especially after the first couple of months, when savings had been used up.[18] Many strike kitchens laid on 500 dinners daily, as well as distributing numerous food parcels. Although preparing food didn't take women away from their traditional roles, many of them learned new skills through having to organise such large-scale operations. As one woman supporter commented:

> During my visits to their kitchen, many would say that they didn't have any particular skills or knowledge whilst sitting in the midst of a busy organisation they themselves had created and were running.[19]

The strike kitchens were politicising in a number of ways. They provided an opportunity for women who would otherwise be stuck passively at home to participate in building the strike:

> I should say honestly, that men would be back at work if it weren't for our women's group. I would have dragged mine back to work. On your own you're under too much pressure, because you've got all the housework to do and no money, and him sitting around all day.[20]

The kitchens became the centre of the community for men, as well as women and children. There they discussed problems and the way forward, and derived a sense of solidarity:

> The kitchens are very important in keeping the community together.

18. The hardship was faced not only with courage but also humour: "We lived on beans. We looked like a bean. It's good job they liked beans." (Quoted in Salt and Layzell 1985, p65.) Much has been written about the hardship the families endured. For further details, refer to the articles cited here from *Spare Rib*, to *Striking Back*, and to Salt and Layzell 1985.
19. Quoted in Dean 1985, p65.
20. Quoted in Campbell 1984, p8.

> They not only provide the main meal of the day, but everyone also comes together and shares their problems and hopes. It is a social function and stops people feeling isolated.[21]

As one striker said: "Coming here you learn more about the strike than you do at most union meetings."[22]

Campaign work

Strike kitchens and welfare work couldn't be run without money, so naturally the raising of funds became a major activity of the women's groups. This meant standing in shopping centres with collection tins, going door to door, running raffles, speaking at workplaces and supporters' functions all over Britain – activities which the vast majority of the women had never even dreamt of before. The experience transformed them and gave them new confidence in themselves. They revelled in their newly discovered abilities and strength.

One example will have to do. It concerns Annette Holroyd, the wife of a miner at Blidworth Colliery near Mansfield, Notts. Annette's mother describes the change in her daughter:

> Before all this, Annette was a nice inoffensive girl who wouldn't say boo to a goose. She was a hard-working housewife, demure, shy even... She was a regular churchgoer... Now she has altered almost beyond recognition. She is a stranger to me now. Sometimes I feel I do not know the person before me.

Annette replied: "Don't be daft, Mam. It's just that I've discovered I'm not the stupid female I always thought I was, that's all".[23]

Women who had never been anywhere without their husbands suddenly found themselves packed off to London, speaking to large audiences, organising rallies and raising money. Though often afraid, they rose to the challenge:

---

21. Robe 1985.
22. Quoted in Callinicos and Simons 1985, p180.
23. Vallely 1985, p10.

The first meeting I ever did was in a college in Oxford. I'd never spoken before in my life – I was shaking like a leaf. I still get the shakes but I do it. Thatcher has had the shock of her life during this strike. She never thought the women could react like this. Before the strike I knew nothing about unions. I didn't want to know.[24]

Many considered the women better at speaking than the men – they argued the case against pit closures better, had facts and figures at their fingertips, and also made a more effective appeal for money to help deal with the hardships the families were enduring. And the transformation the women went through was widely recognised. One Kent miner sums it up:

I'm really proud of my wife, she's been great. She supported me at the start of the strike, just like I knew she would. I didn't expect her to get as involved as she has though. She knows more about the industry – facts and figures – than I do. She's really become more confident in herself since she became involved. Once when I came back from picketing, she was at the door, cases packed, and said, "You'll have to fend for yourself for a few days, I'm off to London," and that was that. I'm really proud of her, she's a good 'un.[25]

A large amount of the money which poured in to finance the strike came from street collections. The act of collecting was politicised by the police as part of their efforts to intimidate the strikers and obstruct their support work. Funds and food boxes were confiscated under manipulated interpretations of vagrancy laws. The Mansfield Labour-controlled local council banned collecting, allowing only "registered charities" to collect in the street.[26]

None of this deterred the collectors. Often the response from the public was rewarding. But not always, as a miner's wife found:

24. Quoted in Callinicos and Simons 1985, p182.
25. Quoted in Dean 1985, p71.
26. Campbell 1984, p8.

> Don't think collecting is easy, it is not. You get abused, called
> horrible names. I've been threatened with being beaten up, shot,
> you name it, I've been called it.[27]

Door-to-door collectors were chased with lawnmowers, or had
dogs set on them.[28]

As well as fundraising and speaking, women's groups
organised rallies and demonstrations. In May 10,000 people
marched through the streets of Barnsley, most of them women.
In August, a mass demonstration in London of Women Against
Pit Closures (WAPC) showed that the women were wholeheartedly with their men, in spite of the media obsession with
violence.

Thousands of women chanted "I'd rather be a picket than
a scab", and "We want 30,000 coppers on the dole".[29] Women
organised local rallies and occupied DHSS offices over the
way welfare was denied to families of strikers, and successfully pressured gas and electricity boards. The demonstrators
presented a petition to the Queen, which was later responded
to by the Energy Minister in a letter addressed not to WAPC, but
to Ann Scargill and Betty Heathfield, wives of NUM officials. It
consisted of attacks on their husbands such as: "Your husbands
have not paid strike pay".[30]

Picketing: "The wives are out!"

During the battle for Nottinghamshire, a car carrying
Yorkshire miners' wives to a picket was stopped at a police
blockade. A policeman looked inside. "Right ladies, on you
go," he said. "We're looking for pickets but we can see you're
not pickets!"[31] The women were proud of their ingenuity
in reaching the pickets. To get through the roadblocks at

27. Arnold 1985, p3. Sometimes there were surprise donors, such as the copper from
    South Wales (Sweeney 1985, p76.)
28. Salt and Layzell 1985, p25.
29. Sweeney 1985, p67; Salt and Layzell 1985, pp36-39.
30. Dobney 1985, p38.
31. Carlin 1984, p5.

3am, they successfully gave all sorts of absurd excuses – they were strippers, or they'd been to a party and lost their friends![32]

Being on a picket line meant a direct experience of the struggle the miners were engaged in. It meant seeing first-hand the forces of the state – the police lined up against the strikers. They experienced taunts and insults from scabs escorted into work by the police. And they understood where the violence so played up by the media came from. Bobby, from the Bentley Women's Action Group in South Yorkshire, described her first experience at a mass picket at Harworth colliery:

> I was petrified. I'd never seen so many police, you just don't in a little village like this. It were a weird feeling. Then, you only have to see one scab and police talking into their machines and down the line goes the whisper, "They're coming", and you just erupt. There was no stopping me, I broke through and got over the other side of the road because it was near scabs... First time on a picket line and I turned two blokes back.[33]

While miners' wives had picketed before, it was never on the scale reached at this strike. Consequently, many were picketing for the first time:

> Now the women in our valley would go on any picket line anywhere they were needed. Not at the beginning of the strike – we wouldn't. Now it's all changed.[34]

Women went to the mass pickets such as Orgreave, as well as their local pickets. They held women-only pickets in many localities. As the strike wore on and the pressure intensified, they showed increasing determination and courage:

> The pigs are policing us with the riot squad also horse and dog

32. Salt and Layzell 1985, p48.
33. Quoted in Loach 1984, p6.
34. Quoted in *Striking Back* 1985, p37.

patrols, but there's one thing we can say, we'll be on the picket lines even if they put tanks there.[35]

And particularly out of the picketing came a new politicisation:

> I think what's hardened a lot of women's attitudes and made them a damn sight more politically aware...is what they've actually experienced with the menfolk getting injured on the picket line.[36]

Other women confirm this. One, when asked whether all the police intimidation had weakened them, replied that without the police, her involvement would have been limited to feeding the kids and fundraising. The police presence hadn't weakened them, she said, rather it had strengthened them.[37] The picketing in particular gave the women the right to say: "We no longer stand behind our men, we stand with them."[38]

Changes in consciousness

Perhaps most commented on by strikers and supporters was the changes in the women's confidence:

> When I look at myself now, I just can't believe I'm the same person. I've grown so big with the knowledge I've got from it. I've never been so motivated to get on with things before. Now there's nothing I can't do, I don't think. Absolutely nothing![39]

The most obvious practical change was to do with housework and childcare. With women active in kitchens and pickets, and away for days on end, men just had to take over some of the domestic responsibilities and the childcare. While men were often reluctant, had to be wheedled into it, or even bribed with sex, there are also frequent stories of men spontaneously doing housework while women were picketing or busy with the

---

35. Bobby and Sue 1984, p4.
36. Harris 1985.
37. From an interview conducted by Penny Green, Cambridge, personal communication.
38. Quoted in Loach 1984, p26.
39. Quoted in Salt and Layzell 1985, p9.

support group. And during the course of the year-long dispute, men who were initially resentful came to understand. Many also helped in the strike kitchens or were even members of women's committees:

> Before if they'd been asked to do those things, they'd have said, "who she bloody talking to?" Now they do it – don't get me wrong, you can't change 'em in 22 weeks, but they do it.[40]

At the end of the strike, many women certainly intended to maintain the new arrangements. As one said, their new understanding of the status of women in the home just couldn't be unlearnt.[41] And another: "Kids, pots and house-work. That's all it were. I think if I had to go back to that I'd jump in t'cut [canal]."[42]

But it was not just housework – men's and women's relationships changed personally and socially. Many wives said they felt closer to their husbands as a result of the strike. Two of many examples: "But in strike we've had loads to talk about. It's really brought us closer." "But now he's more loving towards me. I think he's proud of what I've done during the strike."[43] The sexes mixed more, socially – playing cricket, in the pub, and so on. On the other hand, it was not all plain sailing. Indeed, the financial burdens, constant political activity, police intimidation and pressure from the media placed severe strains on relationships.[44] The women's groups helped many to deal with these stresses – with each other's support they were able to avoid taking everything out in arguments with their husbands. Other women left their husbands because they could stand the strain no longer. But some left for different

---

40. Quoted in Loach 1984, p7.
41. Quoted in Salt and Layzell 1985, p24.
42. Quoted in Salt and Layzell 1985, p24.
43. Salt and Layzell 1985, pp21-24.
44. The extent of these strains can be gauged by the fact that among a workforce of 1,800, at Littleton (Staffordshire), of whom 400 were still on strike in February 1985, 23 marriages are reported to have broken up through the strike. (Doig 1985, p42.)

reasons. One Derbyshire woman tried to persuade her husband not to return to work. But he did. On coming home after the first shift he found her gone, her wedding ring on the kitchen table.[45] Another wife expressed similar views:

> If he went back to work I'd leave him. I'd take the two kids and clear out. I wouldn't live with a scab.[46]

Even the children's lives were changed. They had to go without, of course, but many learned political lessons. At school there were tensions – strikers' kids mixing separately from the kids of those working.[47] Children took to playing "Police and Pickets", instead of Cowboys and Indians; or a game called "The Scabs".[48] New nursery rhymes also appeared:

> *Girls and boys come out to play*
> *The scabs have gone to work today*
> *Sing and dance and do a jig*
> *The NUM will have the pigs.*[49]

One 14-year-old Kent miner's daughter described the changes in her life:

> I think it's brought us closer together, there's been less arguments between the whole family and everyone's really trying to help. We all understand the difficulties with money... In the village everyone's gotten so much closer now. It's nice, like no-one argues with their mum and dad any more.[50]

Some children took the frequent absence of their parents in their stride:

> The kids used to say "Who's going away today? Mummy or Daddy?"[51]

45. Vallely 1985, p10.
46. Quoted in Dean 1985, p61.
47. Kendall et al 1985, p7.
48. *Striking Back* 1985, p38; Salt and Layzell 1985, p41.
49. Quoted in Salt and Layzell 1985, p73.
50. Bense 1984, p27.
51. Quoted in Salt and Layzell 1985, p52.

Others were somewhat resentful:

> They'd say "When are we going to have our Mum back? The same
> Mum we had before the strike?" I've changed that much. But I don't
> think they're ever going to get their old Mum back now.[52]

The problems associated with the children peaked as Christmas neared, and miners' families were upset at the prospect of the children missing out. But the support groups rose to the challenge, and enormous Christmas parties were held, children were given presents, and the already close ties were cemented even further:

> It was marvellous. Fantastic. Incredible. Unbelievable when you
> think about it. They'll never have a Christmas like that again. And
> that's a good thing really because my kids will always remember
> the strike. If only for the Christmas.[53]

Disillusionment and new values

The strike opened up a whole new world of political awareness for women whose lives had previously been so circumscribed. On the one hand, they were now disillusioned with the traditional institutions of society – the media, the courts and, above all, the police. On the other hand, they found themselves newly comprehending the struggles of others, in Ireland and South Africa, of Blacks in Britain; of oppressed groups such as gays; of political issues such as nuclear disarmament; and of the need to link up with other industrial struggles.

Annette Holroyd sums up what an eye-opener the strike was to her:

> It's losing faith in things you once took for granted.
>   The police will no longer be the friendly bobby to me. I will
> always remember the evening when 600 of them surrounded

---

52. Quoted in Salt and Layzell 1985, p23.
53. Quoted in Salt and Layzell 1985, p70.

my house – we counted them – to arrest one of the leaders of the Yorkshire flying pickets who was staying here.

The courts are not what I had assumed. Until now I had never been in one of course. When I did, I heard a magistrate tell a man he was not allowed to speak in his own defence – it had to be done by his solicitor. I did not believe I would hear an accused man silenced in a British court.

I have lost faith in the newspapers I once read. The *Sun* and the *Daily Mirror* are banned from this house now. They are banned from most homes in this village. They have told lies, half-truths, and peddled propaganda.

Even the church has let me down.[54]

Countless women repeat the same loss of faith. But of course, the greatest shock to their minds was the role of the police and the question of violence. Given the extreme behaviour of the police, this is not surprising. As a Welsh miner commented succinctly: "When those coppers started kicking me in the face at Orgreave, well, my attitude changed completely."[55]

Many women naively thought the police would treat them differently, and some thought that perhaps their husbands were exaggerating:

Now we were all very naive, you know, the first morning we went. We thought our men had come back and told us about the police harassment and violence and "Well, we're women, they'll not dare do that to us." Did we get a bloody surprise! We faced the same police harassment as the men, verbal abuse, and the same police violence that our men did. We were no different because we were women.[56]

The violence occurred not just on picket lines but at rallies and in the occupied villages such as Easington in Durham. Police chased small children on their way to school. Old people were

54. Quoted in Vallely 1985, p10.
55. Quoted in *Striking Back* 1985, p182.
56. Quoted in Salt and Layzell 1985, p48.

too petrified to go out of their yards. Police threatened pregnant women, women in wheelchairs.[57] Many ended up with injuries and were hospitalised. Over and over again, the same things were said:

> I never thought I'd see scenes like this in Britain. I never thought I'd see what I've seen on the streets of Easington. We're occupied. We've been occupied by the police. We've had violence in the village. We'll never forget this – never. Not after this.[58]

The abuse from the police literally added insult to injury:

> Call yourself a woman – I wouldn't even piss on you.[59]

The woman was arrested for using foul and abusive language.

The lessons that the women learnt were not just about the "neutrality" of the state and the real role of the police. They were also about the real nature of violence. Although they were scared, their experiences did not turn them into pacifists. They saw that the violence was initiated by the police at the instigation of the government, with political aims in view.

They also found unexpected responses in themselves:

> I'm beginning to see how the violence happens... We regard ourselves as law-abiding people but we were really furious. I can see why our boys get so angry on the picket line and sometimes lose their self-control.[60]

Glynnis Evans, from Maerdy in Wales, saw a small woman being beaten by police:

> I've got no courage but when you saw what they were doing to her you had to do something. I tried to pull away a policeman and said, "get your hands off her", he shouted at me, "get off you, back to your

---

57. Quoted in Salt and Layzell 1985, pp43-51.
58. Quoted in Pattison and Beynon, n.d.
59. Quoted in Huddle et al 1985, p56.
60. Quoted in *Striking Back* 1985, p37.

kitchen sink". I told him, "Yes, I will, and I'll bring it back with me next time and wrap it round your neck!"[61]

To replace lost beliefs in the traditional institutions, the women found a whole new understanding of the world, summed up for some as: "It made me see a truer picture of what capitalism really is."[62] In the past, they might have seen what happened in Ireland, in South Africa, or even in other parts of Britain, as unconnected with themselves. But the strike made them see the connections between different experiences of exploitation and oppression, and the struggles against them.

In June, a Black delegation visited striking miners in Kent. A Black speaker at the joint rally pointed out common interests and stressed the need for solidarity, giving as an example the need to boycott scab coal from South Africa. A Black woman speaker said that, in the past, mining and other working-class communities had not always given support to Blacks in their fight against police harassment. In reply, a miner acknowledged the criticism and said:

> I can assure you all now that the miners will stand behind the Black community against police harassment.[63]

This sort of interaction continued after the strike – Blacks were still collecting money for victimised miners at the Notting Hill Carnival six months later.

Numerous other national groups provided support and raised funds, including Asians, Cypriots and Turks.[64] Ireland,

61. Quoted in Sweeney 1985. These quotes make nonsense of Beatrix Campbell's comment that violence "is a peculiarly masculine characteristic." (Campbell 1985, p22.)
62. Quoted in Salt and Layzell, p74.
63. Bishop 1984, p11.
64. "The Asian community support has been particularly good. 'Now you know what it has been like for us all these years', miners are told." (Rogers 1985, p2). A Greek Cypriot woman commented: "Our community are very sensitive to issues like these, they have a long history of struggle and they relate to it straight away". (Quoted in Loach 1984, p8.)

with its long history of imperialist subjugation, is a crucial issue in Britain. Numerous comments reveal a sense of class solidarity which is a real breakthrough in the British working class. For instance, this is how the wife of a Welsh miner addressed a meeting on Ireland:

> If I had been told nine months ago, before the strike, that I would be here in Oxford speaking on Ireland, I would have told you you were insane. If I had been asked nine months ago whether we lived in a democracy, I would have said yes, on the whole. But I will tell you of many things that have happened during the strike that have left me older and wiser and have shown me how much the working class in this country has in common with the working class in Ireland, how much I as a miner's wife, have in common with a woman in Belfast fighting for her children.[65]

Thatcher had called the miners and their supporters the enemy within. The miners took this up, and stickers appeared everywhere. It epitomised the new level of consciousness that the struggle was not just a narrow and limited sectional one, but one which tended to generalise, which tended to show who were class allies and who was the enemy:

> We knew that one day we had to stand up and fight and we took it in both hands, and my god, we've learned a lot over the last few months. We have discovered that the enemy we face has got many, many heads. It is not just the Coal Board and the DHSS, but the newspapers and the media and the government. And if we are to be the "enemy within", then I'm damned proud to be "the enemy within".[66]

Interactions with the wide network of support groups, and the travelling and speaking necessary to raise funds, meant all

---

65. Quoted in Sweeney 1985, p81.
66. Quoted in Salt and Layzell 1985, p74. Thatcher had said: "In the Falklands we had to fight the enemy without. Here the enemy is within and it is much more difficult to fight but just as dangerous to liberty."

sorts of new experiences beyond the immediate struggle on the picket lines. The most important was the link with other workers through workplace and trade union branch support groups, and solidarity action. And miners and families returned the support from other workers – they stood on picket lines in support of strikes at Barking Hospital, Camden Council and many others.

Support groups not based on workplaces were also very important. Visits and contacts meant new friendships, exposure to different ways of living and new ideas. Responses ranged from accepting new food to planning to stand for parliament. New interests and activities included joining the Labour Party, CND, or (in a minority of cases) revolutionary organisations, or planning actions around hospital closures or local issues. The new experience of travel certainly broadened people's minds. A lot of money and support came from other countries, mainly in Europe.[67] One group, when in Holland, received support not only from trade unionists, but also a group of prostitutes.[68]

Another important spin-off from the struggle was a new link between homosexual groups and miners. Gay men and lesbians were very active in support of the strike, and many mining communities came in contact with open homosexuals for the first time in their lives:

> Before the strike, if I'd known I was going to talk to some lesbians I'd have died. But they're like us. They are normal people... That's something I've learned.[69]

The mining people saw the support gays gave them and, in the course of the struggle, their minds were open to new ideas, as we can see with Sue and Bobby, sisters from Bentley, Yorkshire:

---

67. There are numerous positive examples but one negative example is instructive. The Soviet Union offered free holidays to five families of strikers, but withdrew the offer to two of them on discovering that the couples were not legally married.
68. Seaburne 1985, p6.
69. Quoted in Salt and Layzell 1985, p75.

Sue: Like when the police called you [Bobby] a fucking lesbian on the picket lines you were saying, "I was scared, did he think I was?"...
Bobby: When we talked about it with these feminists they said, "Why be scared, there's nout to be ashamed of" and they put their point to us and it were logical, so I said to young Anne, "your place or mine!"[70]

A gay and lesbian group twinned with a South Wales pit village. When the group visited the village, the organiser admitted he was

a bit apprehensive about how they would be received. But at the welfare social club on the Saturday night, they got a fantastic reception. Of course there were one or two doubting Thomases, but they were quickly dealt with. A miner's wife at one table tore a strip off a miner who complained about the visit. She told him in no uncertain terms, that people's sex lives were their own business. The table supported her.[71]

The response went beyond simple acceptance of homosexuals to political support for them. The Notts Women's Support Group wrote to the London Lesbians and Gay Men Support the Miners Group:

We also extend to you our total solidarity and support in your struggle against all forms of oppression and prejudice on the grounds of sexuality. Our struggles are part and parcel of the same fight.[72]

Three months after the strike, a substantial contingent of miners participated in the London demonstration in Gay Pride Week.

---

70. Quoted in Loach 1984, p26.
71. Quoted in Rose 1984, p12.
72. Quoted in *Solidarity with the Miners* 1985, p29.

Sexism and the limitations of the action groups

It would be foolish to pretend that the struggle consisted only of strengths and blinding transformations of consciousness. There was sexism among the miners. Within the women's groups themselves there were problems and, despite a high level of activism, too many women remained passively at home. While many women were politicised, the activity of others tended to reproduce their traditional roles – cooking, caring for children, playing a back-up role in pickets.

But it would be wrong to see the difficulties simply as a consequence of sexism. The reality is more complex, and many of the problems of organisation are related to the general problems of the strike rather than specific to the women's committee.

To deal with sexism first. It cannot be a surprise to anyone that in the tradition-bound, isolated mining communities men (and women) had traditional views of male and female roles. This sexism expressed itself sometimes in reluctance to share housework. But many men changed, as has been discussed already. It also expressed itself in half-joking fears about feminists the women might meet while on speaking tours, and warnings not to pick up any of their "strange ideas".[73] Perhaps most galling was when women courageously appeared on picket lines only to be greeted with comments such as "Get your tits up for the lads". But many of the women's group members took the minority of men who did this to task:

> Yes, they'd shout things on picket lines and we'd go up and say, "we're not here for stuff like that." It makes 'em think.[74]
>
> These issues have to be tackled head on. We are making every effort to take an equal part in winning this strike and we must

---

73. For example Maerdy (South Wales) women when visiting Oxford.
74. Quoted in Loach 1984, p26.

demand not only for ourselves but that all women be treated as equals.[75]

The fact is, while all agreed that change couldn't happen overnight, and while some men couldn't or wouldn't change, an impulse for change *did* come out of the struggle:

> Miners are brought up in a very chauvinistic way, but since the strike many attitudes have changed... I've heard lads say, "cor, that Margaret, she's a bloody good worker isn't she?" and they would never refer to her in any other way. Now before the strike, they would be saying "she's not a bad looker, is she? I wonder who is knocking about with her?" But it's different now, it's not sexist language that gets used now when they refer to a woman.[76]

More serious than passing comments or pin-ups in the union paper were the difficulties sometimes put in the way of women trying desperately to become active. There were, for example, a number of problems in South Wales.[77] Men in one village jealously guarded their kitchen from a newly formed women's group, tried to stop women meeting and put pressure on individual women to stop them from joining the group. A large women's rally met with opposition because they did not go through "proper channels". Various obstacles were put in the way of women getting to pickets and rallies. Officials did their best to prevent them from going to Port Talbot pickets because it would be "too dangerous" for women, and "they would just get in the way". Another official responded to the suggestion that more should be done to mobilise women by saying that they were just a nuisance.

Some of this is simple sexism, and it is evidence of the women breaking out of their traditional passivity that they

---

75. Douglas 1984, p11. It must also be pointed out that male NUM members also opposed such sexist remarks, produced leaflets, and raised the issue on the picket line. ("Learning From the Strike", p9.)
76. Quoted in Dean 1985, p70.
77. Jackson 1984, p9.

didn't just buckle under; they didn't ask the men for permission to be involved, they just did it. But there is also evidence here of a characteristic of this strike – a desire by officials to keep everything under control and to discourage independent rank-and-file activity. The obstacles the women came up against were also experienced by miners when it came to picketing and making direct contact with other workers and potential supporters. The officials kept tight control over picketing. Later in the strike, they didn't organise the mass pickets so necessary for victory, but relied on token pickets of six in compliance with court orders. The national leadership was not very keen on twinning either, until well into the strike. It meant funds going directly to pits, bypassing central control.

There are other examples which have been interpreted as sexist but which are really illustrative of the general problems of this strike. Take for instance two cases: the Yorkshire men who rebuffed women wishing to join picket lines with "It's our job, it's our fight, it's our picket",[78] and the NUM meeting which turned out a 10-year-old boy because they wouldn't discuss strike matters in front of non-members.[79] Both these instances exemplify not maleness but narrow-minded sectionalism, an approach for which a Welsh miner criticised his union officials:

> The NUM didn't get solidarity because the executive kept saying it was a miners' strike and we didn't need other workers on the picket line... We got offers from [various workers] to come onto the picket line. But the union said it was to be miners only. They didn't even like miners' wives on the picket line at first.[80]

Much of the obstructionism the women encountered can therefore be considered not sex-specific, but a consequence of official bureaucracy and narrow sectionalist industrial politics.

---

78. Campbell 1984.
79. Loach 1984, p8.
80. Quoted in Callinicos and Simons 1985, p214.

Passivity and bureaucratism

Again, it was not all sweetness and light within the women's groups. They were extremely varied – some had no democratic structure, while others were so democratic that "they were almost inoperable".[81] They made mistakes. But this is only to be expected in a spontaneous movement composed largely of totally inexperienced people.

But there was a more fundamental problem. In spite of the mass mobilisation of women into activity, large numbers remained passive. There were some straightforward explanations – young children, jobs, or living in isolated villages. But nonetheless many, although supporting the strike, didn't become active themselves. This passivity often meant that a comparatively small number of women came to dominate the action groups. The Mill Hill Women's Support Group in Kent is an example. Due to the lack of active participation, a small number found themselves running the activities of the group. Not only did they do the day-to-day work of the strike kitchens, they also went on speaking tours and organised rallies. The consequent domination by a small active group intimidated others, who stayed away.

> The group is dominated by a group of very strong women, they are too outspoken. I feel very intimidated by them. I once tried to get involved but when I made suggestions they were largely ignored. They felt I had no right to criticise the way they were running things. I was only trying to help so that the group could run more effectively.
>
> They organise everything, when you try to give a hand they boss you around. There are a lot of us who think the group could run a lot better than it does but we don't want to cause any trouble.

The passive group of women maintained contact with each other through an informal network. They supported the strike,

---

81. Quoted in Salt and Layzell 1985, p8.

but failed to break out of their traditional roles. They would perhaps have liked to be more involved but didn't know how:

> That group should be more democratic, I would like to be able to go up there and say what I really think and feel about the way things are being run, but I can't, they are too overpowering for me... I just don't know what we are supposed to do to make the group work better.[82]

The Mill Hill group was not exceptional. The problem of passivity was experienced by men and women in all areas. The 1972 strike had been won by rank-and-file organising of mass pickets, which generated the support of other workers, particularly Birmingham engineering workers. In 1984/85, rank-and-file preparedness to organise independently was lacking. As a result of the passivity of many, and the dominance of the women's groups by a small number, the women's groups remained very much under the influence of the bureaucracy – despite their determination to remain independent of the NUM. This was evident at the wives' march in London in August 1984. The march was led by Ann Scargill and Betty Heathfield, wives of the union's secretary and president. Female trade union officials ordered the tops of *Socialist Worker* placards to be removed, and every effort was made to depoliticise the event.[83]

The influence of the union bureaucracy became particularly clear when, during the northern summer of 1984, the emphasis in the official strategy of the strike turned more toward winning public support rather than adopting the militant tactics necessary to win. If you are aiming at public sympathy, women and children can be very useful.

But here we see a massive contradiction. On the one hand, women feel they are taking a positive step forward into collective activity with other women. On the other hand, they remain tied to traditional work, food and childcare in the village, and

---

82. Information and quotes on problems in the Mill Hill group from Dean 1985, pp58-71.
83. "Miners' Wives" 1984, p7.

symbols of suffering families in public. Thus, the organisation of miners' wives never really broke with the traditional ideas about the role of women.

The women's organisation mirrored the passivity and weaknesses of the strike as a whole. This led to continued domination by the union bureaucrats and a tendency in practice to reinforce the traditional female role. On the other hand, the women's organisation showed the potential for working-class women to break out of that role.

Feminism and blinkered politics

Activists in the women's movement in Britain generally ignored or minimised the struggles of working-class women in the years leading up to the strike, concentrating instead on separatist and pacifist activities such as the Greenham Common Women's Peace Camp. But the miners' strike suddenly changed that. Many feminists abandoned or modified their separatism in practice.[84]

> For many feminists, the miners' strike has meant reassessing our attitudes to working with men and has shown the real links between feminism and the struggles of working-class women.[85]

While retaining their opposition to traditional male and female roles, they felt for example, that it would look "arrogant to impose our 'ideologically sound' selection of toys on children regardless of choice".[86]

However, separatism still retained a strong ideological hold. This can be seen for instance in the separate support

---

84. I am using the term here to mean women who believe that the fundamental divide in society is between men and women. However, I am only concerned with feminists broadly speaking on the left. I do not feel it necessary to answer the "supporter" who wrote to *Spare Rib* as follows: "But you ignore those women whose husbands decide to go to work (in the pits) – what moral support do such women get from other women? What about feminist policewomen? Feminist Conservatives? They need our support just as much." (Miller 1984)

85. Withal 1984, p31.

86. Sweeney 1985, p83.

groups for women which were set up in many areas. There are practical objections to such separate groups – double the meetings, for example.[87] But the feminist approach led to a blinkered politics, which impeded a genuine understanding of the nature of the strike and, in particular, led to a fundamental contradiction between the feminists and the mining women they were supporting.

The feminists make the women the centre of their strategy. They separate them out, distinguish their activity in a fundamental way from the "tough men doing the 'real' political stuff",[88] and lay emphasis on the way the mining women have organised politically as women. This is in sharp contrast to the mining women themselves. While they were very conscious of being women (which consciousness after all is a product of the separate roles), they were impelled into the struggle precisely because of a desperately felt need for unity with their men. The pit closures would mean the end of whole communities, and the whole community – women, men and children – responded to the threat.

In the miners' strike, tens of thousands of women were fighting and organising for the first time precisely because they were wives. It was the struggle itself which forced them to confront their female role and, in many cases, to break out of it. Thus, while they often came into conflict with men over sexist behaviour, there was no tendency towards feminist separatism. Shoulder to shoulder unity was their aim:

> It has also given us the strength to stand side by side with our men, fighting with them and, in some cases fighting against them for the right to stand on picket lines with them.[89]

The feminists' determination to see everything from the women's point of view assumed that there *was* a distinct

---

87. Sweeney 1985, p89.
88. Lambeth Women's Miners' Support Group, pp32-33.
89. Quoted in Lambeth Women's Miners' Support Group, pp32-33.

women's point of view in this struggle, that men and women had different objectives, and that the women's objectives were (or should be) those conventionally accepted within the women's movement. As a result, they often failed to see the actual point of view of the women of the mining communities. For example, in meetings on the strike, feminists repeatedly asked why the miners' wives weren't demanding the right to go down the pits. But most wives don't want to work in the mines any more than the feminists themselves want to.[90]

There were disagreements over songs and slogans which the mining women didn't see as sexist, and occasionally there was more serious conflict:

> I had a row with this woman in London – she said it's our fault that our men are male chauvinists. But that's not true. Our men are male chauvinists because it's been bred into them.[91]

And at the end, although they had a new-found sense of their own independence and worth and plans for the future, the women had no intention of leaving their families for separatist-type reasons.

These differences didn't cause serious problems during the white heat of the struggle. But in assessing the strike, we have to look at the political lessons. A politics which is based on an assumption of a separate women's point of view has certain consequences. On the one hand, it inhibits an understanding of the real lessons of this struggle, lessons essentially the same for women as for men: the role of the trade union officials, the need for independent rank-and-file action, the need to counter passivity, the necessity of mass picketing and solidarity to win. On the other hand, the logic of centring on women is to see men as the enemy. And such a politics is incapable of providing a theoretical basis for the liberation of women.

One example of the first consequence is the tendency to

---

90. Carlin 1985.
91. Quoted in Salt and Layzell, p21.

see sexism in incidents involving men, when what is really involved are (as discussed above) questions of bureaucratism or sectionalism. The question of violence, however, provides us with an example which illustrates both consequences well.

Some feminists made strong efforts to relate Greenham Common to the strike.[92] Activists from the peace camp joined miners' picket lines, and many wives expressed admiration for their struggle. But Beatrix Campbell, a well-known feminist and member of the British Communist Party, took this much further, and attempted to draw ideological conclusions. Campbell was already known for having caricatured miners as the most sexist section of male society one month before the strike, in her *Wigan Pier Revisited*. In her articles on the strike, Campbell appeared particularly upset about "chaotic macho violence".[93] She advocated instead, as a way of achieving tactical aims and avoiding injury, non-violent direct action as used by Greenham Common women.

There are two points here. Firstly, there is the question of whether pacifist methods do work. When women from the peace camp (experienced and trained as Campbell advocates) did go on a picket line, they found their sit-down pacifist tactics were not superior:

> The [Greenham Common and other] women led the blockade in an attempt to prevent lorries from leaving. They sat in the road and were then joined by several miners who were brutally treated by the police.[94]

---

92. Loach 1984, p6.
93. Campbell 1985. I only have space here to consider one aspect of Campbell's politics. For a critique of her politics on women, see German 1985. For a more general discussion of the politics of the Eurocommunist wing of the Communist Party to which Campbell belongs, including its attitude to the miners' strike, see Callinicos 1985.
94. "Miners Support" 1984, p9. Compare with Campbell's contemptuous comment: "It's as if lying down is something inherently threatening to the virility of class warriors." (Campbell 1984.)

But more important is the question of Campbell's condemnation of the "macho violence" on both sides. To condemn
the picketers in this way is to follow the unsavoury lead of
Neil Kinnock, with his craven capitulation to media lies and
hysteria.

Campbell was able to find some miners' wives who criticised the violence on the picket lines, but this proves nothing.
The overwhelming majority of the comments indicate that
women came to understand the cause to be the police, and did
not consider it to be "male violence". All accounts by the picketers (male and female) at Port Talbot, Orgreave or any other
picket line make it quite clear that the police were prepared
and armed, that they initiated attacks, that their aim was to
beat and terrify the picketers. The picketers themselves had
essentially political aims. In Notts, the main aim was to talk to
the working miners to try to persuade them to join the strike. At
Orgreave, the aim was to prevent shipment of coke, and later in
the strike it was stopping scabs entering the mines. But because
of the police strategies, self-defence was frequently necessary.
When pickets engaged in mass confrontations with police over
scabs, such as at Easington, this was a necessary part of the
struggle and had nothing to do with maleness. Furthermore,
the violence that occurred in the mining villages (such as the
notorious occasion at Grimethorpe when police attacked men,
women and children picking coal on the colliery tip) was wholly
the responsibility of the police. To condemn all men together
as hopelessly violent is clearly to argue that men are collec-
tively the enemy. It follows from this that we should unite all
women, including Margaret Thatcher (who of course, for her
own reasons, condemned violence as "totally unacceptable in
our society"). And a failure to distinguish the police violence
and its political purpose from the miners' violence and its role
in the struggle shows a total inability to understand the class
forces at work in the strike.

Conclusion

At the end of the strike, the miners were forced to return to work without a settlement. They were defeated, having achieved neither the aim of the strike – the prevention of pit closures – nor the protection of victimised workers. But it was a pyrrhic victory for Thatcher: she had spent over £3 billion without achieving her aim – the destruction of the NUM. The men and women of the pit villages, and their thousands of supporters around Britain, felt that although the specific aims of the strike had not been attained, it had nonetheless been a major achievement and, as so many said, things would never be the same again.

But in assessing the strike and its significance for women, it is important not to glamorise the women's participation or ignore the weaknesses. The conclusions I will draw are different from those drawn by many others.

Some people have tried to argue that an entirely new women's movement emerged during the conflict, which will now go on to bigger and better things. The facts do not support this argument. It is true that WAPC has continued since the return to work. Many groups are active around union issues (such as victimised miners and the breakaway Notts branch), or local community issues, and over 700 women attended a national conference in August.

But there are problems. The level of participation has dropped sharply and, in the villages, women are just not coming to meetings. At the conference, there was a serious conflict over voting rights which was largely between rank-and-file activists and union officialdom (represented by officials' wives).[95]

It does not belittle the heroic struggle waged by the women of the British mining communities to admit that this is not the first time such a thing has happened. Women in British

---

95. Waterson 1985; Wintour 1985; Fran and Leili 1985, p4.

coalfields have a tradition of supporting industrial action.[96] In American mining areas at the turn of the century, Mother Jones and her "wild women" were famous, and the Australian Miners Women's Auxiliary played a leading role in the 1930s.[97]

It is true that the extent and scope of the women's role in this struggle was unprecedented. But it has to be understood not as something entirely new but, rather, as something building on previous struggles in mining communities and other recent activities of British women workers, such as at Grunwicks, Lee Jeans and many others.

So a fundamentally new movement was not created. And it would be utopian to expect WAPC to continue in the way it was before, as a mass movement. With the strike now over, the focus which mobilised people into activity is no longer there.

Another common argument about the strike says that the men saw it in traditional industrial terms, supposedly now demonstrated to have been inadequate, and to this are counter-posed "new methods" developed by the women which show the way forward.[98]

I do not have space to discuss here the issue of the traditional methods. But I would argue that, even given all their creativity and transformations of consciousness, it is wrong to draw different conclusions from the activity of the women and that of the men. On the contrary, their activities tended to converge in the course of the struggle. We have seen that men started to take over housework and childcare, while women went on speaking tours and joined in picket lines, and a new respect was born for each other's work.

---

96. Carlin 1984 discusses the history of the participation of women in coalfields struggles.

97. See Stone 2008 for more information on the Australian Miners Women's Auxiliary. See also Mother Jones 1976.

98. This unfortunately seems to be the position taken by Lyn Beaton in her otherwise very good article on her experiences in Blidworth during the strike (Beaton 1985, p4).

The common fight for the common goal led to changes in both sexes and a tendency for gender divisions to break down. This should not be overstated. The point is that it shows how it is possible for the sexual division of labour to be overcome – it is a pointer for the future.

In a similar way, many of the problems and weaknesses were not sex-specific, but the result of the general weaknesses of the strike – passivity, and reliance on the union bureaucracy. This, again, shows the way in which women did not have differing needs and interests in the dispute, but had the same lessons to learn.

The importance of this strike, then, is not just for the immediate issues that come out of it, but for the way in which it shows that people can change in the course of struggle, and the possibility for that struggle to be united. It is on this possibility that I base my belief in the possibility of socialism and women's liberation.

References

Arnold, Brenda 1985, "Wife on a mission of mercy", *Right of Reply Special*.

Beaton, Lyn 1985, "Women in the British miners' strike: wives or warriors?" *Scarlet Woman*, 20, Spring.

Bense, Ellie 1984, *Spare Rib*, 147, October. (*Spare Rib* archive available at https://journalarchives.jisc.ac.uk/britishlibrary/sparerib#browse.)

Bishop, Marla 1984, "Black delegation to Kent miners", *Spare Rib*, 145, August.

Bobby and Sue 1984, letter, *Spare Rib*, 149, December.

Callinicos, Alex 1985, "The politics of *Marxism Today*", *International Socialism*, 2:29, Summer. https://www.marxists.org/history/etol/ writers/callinicos/1985/xx/marxtoday.html.

Callinicos, Alex and Mike Simons 1985, *The Great Strike* (special double issue of *International Socialism*, 2:27/28), Socialist Worker. https://www. marxists.org/history/etol/writers/callinicos/1985/miners/index.html.

Campbell, Beatrix 1984, "The other miners' strike", *New Statesman*, 27 July.

Campbell, Beatrix 1985, "Politics old and new", *New Statesman*, 8 March.

Carlin, Norah 1984, "Wives, mothers and fighters", *Socialist Review*, 66, June. https://www.marxists.org/history/etol/writers/carlin/1984/06/wives. html.

Carlin, Norah 1985, "Feminism & the miners' strike: towards a new unity?" *Socialist Worker Review*, 72, January.

Dean, Dixie 1985, "The 1984/85 miners' strike and the mining communities of the East Kent coalfields", unpublished BSc Hons Thesis, City University, London.

Dobney, Megan 1985, "Walker says husbands to blame for strike!", in *Right of Reply Special*.

Doig, Jim 1985 "Our pride has taken us so far", in *Right of Reply Special*.

Douglas, Maureen 1984, "Mining for change", *Spare Rib*, 144, July.

Fran and Leili 1985, "Going forward: women against pit closures", *Outwrite*, 39, September.

German, Lindsay 1985, "Women workers: victims of the class struggle?", *Socialist Worker Review*, 73, February.

Harris, Ann 1985, "We'll stand up and speak up for ourselves", in Kendall et al.

Hollingsworth, Mark 1984, "Using miners to bust the union", *New Statesman*, 14 December.

Huddle, Roger, Angela Phillips, Mike Simons and John Sturrock 1985, *Blood, sweat and tears: Photographs from the great miners' strike 1984-1985*, Artworker Books.

Jackson, Stevie 1984, "Behind men? not quite!", *Spare Rib*, 146, September.

Kendall, Tina, Rachel Lever and Barbara Norden 1985, "What did you do in the strike, mum?", *Spare Rib*, 151, February.

Lambeth Women's Miners' Support Group 1985, "Striking new connections", *Spare Rib*, 153, April.

"Learning from the strike" (interview with a group of SWP miners) 1985, *Socialist Worker Review*, 74, March.

Loach, Loretta 1984, "We'll be here right to the end", *Spare Rib*, October.

Miller, KAW 1984, "Don't get me wrong", letter, *Spare Rib*, 149, December.

"Miners Support" 1984, *Spare Rib*, 146, September.

"Miners' Wives" 1984, *Socialist Worker Review*, 68, September.

Mother Jones 1976, *The autobiography of Mother Jones*, Charles H Kerr.

Pattison, Keith, and Huw Beynon nd, 1984 *Easington August '84*, A SIDE publication, Newcastle.

Right of Reply Special 1985, produced by workers on the *Sun* and *News of the World*, London and Manchester, March.

Robe, E 1985, "Women fight for the future", *Right of Reply Special*.

Rogers, Nick 1985, "Where being on strike takes guts", *Right of Reply Special*.

Rose, John 1984, "Sister, brother and twin", *New Statesman*, 30 November.

Salt, Chrys and Jim Layzell 1985, *Here we go! Women's memories of the 1984/85 miners' strike*, London Political Committee Co-Operative Retail Services.

Seaburne, Tish 1985, "Weekend in Wales", in Kendall et al.

Solidarity with the Miners 1985, Labour Research Department, London.

Stone, Janey 2008, "Brazen hussies and God's police. Fighting back in the depression years", in Sandra Bloodworth and Tom O'Lincoln (eds), *Rebel Women in Australian Working Class History*, Red Rag Publications. https://sa.org.au/interventions/rebelwomen/brazen.htm.

Striking Back 1985, WCCPL and NUM, South Wales Area.

Sweeney, Anne-Marie 1985, "The Oxford Women's Support Group", in Alan Thornett (ed), *The Miners' Strike in Oxford*, Oxford and District TUC, Oxford.

Vallely, Paul 1985, "The strike that turned wives into warriors", *The Times*, 4 March.

Waterson, Julie 1985, "Opportunity knocked", *Socialist Worker*, 21 August.

Wintour, Patrick 1985, "Women pledge to sustain fight against pit closures", *The Guardian*, 19 August.

Withal, Debbie 1984, "Manchester Women's Support Conference", in Kendall et al 1985.

IAN BIRCHALL

The Comintern's encounter with syndicalism

Ian Birchall is a writer and translator in London, UK. He has written books on Babeuf and Sartre, and a biography of Tony Cliff, and has translated Alfred and Marguerite Rosmer and Victor Serge. For many years a member of the British Socialist Workers Party, he is now not attached to any organisation, but still considers himself a revolutionary socialist.

I T IS NOW over a hundred years since the Russian Revolution and the subsequent foundation of the Communist International (Comintern) in 1919. The Comintern was created in response to a wave of revolt which swept across Europe (and to some extent other parts of the world) in the aftermath of the First World War. Sickened by four years of slaughter in the trenches, and angry at the corrupt and incompetent rulers who had sent them to die there, working people were enthused by the news of the Bolshevik victory.

Often they knew few details of what was happening in Russia. But what was important was a feeling of hope – hope that the old order was doomed to perish and that a new form of society based on equality and cooperation was coming into being. Learned disquisitions which dissect the minutiae of the rise of communism, but forget the fundamental factor of hope, fail to understand the dynamic that drove the whole process.

Lenin and the Bolshevik leaders knew that without support from workers elsewhere in the world the revolution was doomed to failure. Fourteen foreign armies had been sent into Russia to try to overthrow the new regime. But the Bolsheviks faced a fundamental problem. In 1914 a powerful and well-organised working-class movement had existed in Europe; but the vast majority of its leadership had opted to support the war, often joining pro-war governments with right-wing bourgeois parties. A new leadership was urgently needed to give shape and organisation to the rising revolt.

So the aim of the newly-founded Comintern was to create new parties which would break with the old organisations fatally compromised by their support for the war. It had to be done quickly – the fate of the Russian Revolution would be decided within just a few years. Initially there were signs of hope. In 1919 Communists took power, albeit briefly, in Hungary and Bavaria. Things moved very quickly. The Hungarian Communist Party was only founded in November 1918; by the following March it was in power. The next years saw a wave of factory occupations in Italy and a general strike in France. Between 1918 and 1923 Germany seemed to be hovering on the brink of revolution.

Later historians may look back and argue that the hopes of spreading the revolution were exaggerated. But life is not lived in retrospect; at the time the Bolsheviks and their allies elsewhere in the world believed they had a reasonable chance of success. They were only too well aware that if they failed there would be a new wave of reaction. Everything was at stake. This is the context in which both the achievements and the mistakes of the Comintern should be studied.

For many years the left, and especially its revolutionary wing, has stood in the shadow of the Comintern. It represented the highest point of struggle and organisation that the working-class movement had reached thus far, and so seemed to be a model to emulate. For many years Trotskyist organisations used to take pride in standing in the tradition of the "first four congresses of the Communist International" – that is, the years 1919-1922, when Lenin and Trotsky had played a leading role in the Comintern.

Yet the history of the Comintern has often been more invoked than understood. The rise of Stalin marked a sharp break in the Comintern's history – many of those who had played a key role in the early years disappeared, either voluntarily or through expulsion. Most histories were written either by those who saw Stalin's USSR as the legitimate heir of Leninism, or by Cold War apologists who viewed Leninism and Stalinism with equal hostility and failed to distinguish between them.

So it is only in recent years, with the end of the Cold War and the availability of the Russian archives, that it has been possible to get a more accurate picture of the reality of the Comintern. A team of researchers headed by John Riddell have produced the full minutes of the first four congresses, offering a more complex picture than was previously available.[1] Pierre Broué's history of the Comintern, based on formidable erudition, combines a commitment to its basic values with a clear-sighted recognition of its weaknesses.[2] Important histories of the early years of the French and German Communist Parties have opened up new perspectives on their origins.[3]

We no longer look to the Comintern as a model for imitation; our revolution, if and when we make it, will be substantially different from October 1917. But that does not mean there is nothing to be learned from history. History involves both continuity and change, and a movement that is aware of its own past is better armed to make its future. In that spirit I want to look at one particular theme, the relation between the Comintern and revolutionary syndicalism.

Most accounts of the collapse of the European labour movement in 1914 tend to focus on the Second International, founded in 1889 with the encouragement of Engels. True, the Second International had within its membership the leading Marxists – Lenin and Luxemburg as well as Kautsky – and the main reformist leaders. But a substantial number of European and North American workers owed their allegiance to revolutionary syndicalism, which was well implanted in

---

1. Riddell 1987, Riddell 1991, Riddell 2011, Riddell 2015.
2. Broué 1997.
3. Chuzeville 2017, Ferrette 2011, Cyr 2013, Fernbach 2011, Frölich 2013.

France, Italy, Spain, Britain, Ireland and the USA.[4] And the influence spread wider; one of the leading Bolshevik worker-intellectuals, Shlyapnikov, spent years working in France and came into contact with syndicalist ideas.[5]

It is important to be clear about what syndicalism was. Often the word has been used almost as a term of abuse. In Russia the Workers' Opposition was denounced for "syndicalism". More recently it has often been used to indicate an excessive preoccupation with trade-union activity at the expense of "politics".

The syndicalism of the pre-1914 labour movement was somewhat more complex. French syndicalism, which had a considerable influence elsewhere, was embodied in the trade-union organisation the Confédération Générale du Travail (General Confederation of Labour – CGT), founded in 1895. The basic principles of syndicalism were set out in the Charter of Amiens of 1906, which argued that trade-union organisation should be independent of any political organisation. It stated that "for syndicalism to achieve its maximum effect, economic action must be carried out directly against the bosses, the confederated organisations not having to involve themselves, as a union group, with parties and sects that can, outside and alongside, pursue social transformation in complete freedom". The individual member was warned "to not introduce into the union the opinions he professes outside it".[6] Émile Pouget, one of the main founding figures of French syndicalism, put it rather more bluntly – "Politics, we don't need it! So if you really must, go and do it in the shithouse!"[7]

Pouget, together with Émile Pataud, wrote *Comment nous ferons la révolution* (How We Shall Make The Revolution, 1909), which, in form of a novel, imagined the transition to a socialist

---

4. See Darlington 2008.
5. Allen 2016.
6. Charter of Amiens 1906.
7. Cited in Dubief 1969, p70.

society: an army attack on workers led to a general strike, the dissolution of parliament and the taking over of all economic and social functions by the trade unions. A counter-revolution-ary invasion was repulsed. The unions, and the unions alone, provided all the organisation and leadership necessary.

But when the syndicalists dismissed "politics", they meant, essentially, the activities of political parties, and in particular their involvement in parliamentary elections. They did not mean more general political considerations about the organ-isation of society. Alfred Rosmer, one of the most perceptive writers associated with pre-1914 French syndicalism, later attempted to analyse this.

He argued that French syndicalism was a reaction against the Second International model of organisation, whereby the labour movement was divided into a political wing and an economic wing, which divided their responsibilities between them. He described this as

> the direct legacy of the decrepit, thoroughly rotten and mendacious Second International, whose principle was as follows: "You shall concern yourself with political matters and we with economic matters; don't stick your nose in our affairs and we won't worry about yours".[8]

In Rosmer's terms this meant that the CGT was a "hybrid" organisation, in that it functioned both as a trade union and as a political party at the same time. This had the advantage of avoiding an artificial separation between economic and politi-cal issues. But it also entailed certain disadvantages. Because the CGT played the role of a party as well as of a union, it was more difficult for it to present itself as the organisation of all the employed, regardless of political or ideological differences, as the unions in Britain and Germany did. As a result, union-isation levels in France were much lower than in Britain or Germany – half a million members in France compared to four

---

8. Rosmer 1921, p70.

million trade unionists in Britain. The union came to be seen, not as the organisation of the whole class, but as an "active minority". So when the union took the initiative in a strike or campaign, other non-unionised workers would follow its lead. (This tradition of minority unionism has persisted in France – in May 1968, during the biggest general strike in human history to that point, at least seven million out of the ten million strikers were not unionised.)

Although there were differences between syndicalism and anarchism, the syndicalist tradition owed something to anarchism. Whereas Marxism had focused on exploitation as the fundamental basis of class conflict, anarchism and syndicalism tended to put greater emphasis on the principle of authority. This could be a weakness but it could also be a strength. While the concept of exploitation was central to an understanding of the economic mechanisms of capitalism, the question of authority related more directly to the day-to-day experience of workers. In the workplace workers did not immediately experience the falling rate of profit, but rather the harshness and bullying of their manager or supervisor.

There was a strong moral current in syndicalism, in contrast to the more "scientific" pretensions of Marxism. One form taken by this was the principle of what the French syndicalists called the "*refus de parvenir*" (the refusal to make a career). An example of this was Maurice Dommanget, a founding member of the French Communist Party and one of the finest historians of his generation, who could have held a university post, but preferred to remain as a primary school teacher and trade-union activist.

But the syndicalist tradition did have serious weaknesses. These had already become apparent at the end of the nineteenth century, during the notorious Dreyfus affair, when a Jewish army officer was falsely accused of spying and exiled to Devil's Island in French Guiana. Because of their predominant emphasis on class, many syndicalists argued that workers had no interest in defending a wealthy officer and that they should not take sides. There was anti-Semitism among the syndicalists, but primarily this was a question of stressing class to the exclusion of other forms of oppression. (Many of the Socialist leaders, like Jaurès, were equally slow to respond).

Likewise, with their emphasis on class struggle in the workplace, many syndicalists tended to ignore or give little importance to the question of women's oppression. In 1912 in France there was the notorious case of Mme Couriau, who took a job in the printing industry. The union not only refused her membership, but expelled her husband for failing to persuade her to quit her job! Fortunately some syndicalists, notably Alfred Rosmer, spoke out vigorously against this.

But though there were serious weaknesses in the syndicalist tradition, syndicalists were in the forefront of struggle in several countries. In the United States the Industrial Workers of the World (IWW) were at the centre of many conflicts. In the Lawrence Massachusetts textile workers' strike of 1912 there were 23,000 strikers speaking at least 14 different languages; by organising mass pickets and daily demonstrations with up to ten thousand participants, the IWW led the strikers to victory.

In Spain syndicalist Francisco Ferrer was well-known for setting up a network of independent, secular libertarian schools. He was executed on trumped up charges in 1909 following a week of insurrection in Barcelona, and there were militant demonstrations throughout Europe.

In France the syndicalists found themselves confronted with a violent and brutal state. The Clemenceau government had come to power on the basis of support for Dreyfus, but on several occasions used the army to break strikes, and strikers were shot. On one occasion most of the CGT leadership were arrested and imprisoned.

But precisely the confrontation with the state meant that the CGT had to develop a political as well as a trade-union response. One very important aspect of this was the way the

CGT developed an anti-militarist strategy. Opposition to the use of the army for strike-breaking was one important aspect of this approach, but syndicalist anti-militarism went far beyond this. The possibility of a war with Germany, developing into a Europe-wide conflict with massive destruction, was part of the consciousness of many French workers. In 1910 syndicalist Alphonse Merrheim asked:

> What will be necessary to make France go to war? To persuade it that it is in danger, that national rights have been trampled underfoot. .... Our chauvinistic press, well bribed, will find it easy to howl that French intervention is necessary.[9]

In 1902 the CGT published a pamphlet called the *Nouveau Manuel du Soldat* (the New Soldier's Manual). This set out briefly the anti-militarist case, with arguments and quotations from various writers. Some 200,000 copies were distributed. The target audience was young men who were being called up for military service. The *Manuel* left it to their discretion what they should do – if they found the pressures of military life insupportable they should desert, but if they felt able to stay in the army and argue with their fellow-conscripts they should do that. But at all costs they should refuse to shoot on their fellow-workers.

But the CGT went beyond propaganda with the establishment of the *sou du soldat* (soldier's *sou* – a *sou* was a coin of very low value, perhaps one hundredth of a day's wage). A fund was created from contributions from trade-union members which was used to send to conscripts a small sum of money and some propaganda – the aim was to provide a few luxuries which might make their miserable existence more tolerable, but also to maintain contact between soldiers and the trade-union movement (by, for example, inviting them to visit the local trade-union centre). It was hoped to build up a body of anti-militarist activists within the conscript army.

9. Merrheim 1911.

Of course the numbers involved were far too small to take effective action in the event of war. But the anti-militarist agitation was sufficient to cause a certain degree of anxiety in government circles. The number of desertions increased, although not dramatically. When the primary teachers' union voted to support the *sou du soldat* in 1912, there was considerable alarm.

There were different currents of opinion within the syndicalist movement, and many activists had an essentially reformist position. The most politically developed current was that around the journal *La Vie ouvrière* (Workers' Life). Launched in 1909, this was inspired and edited by the remarkable militant Pierre Monatte, and appeared twice a month. It was aimed at what one might describe as worker intellectuals – trade-union activists with little formal schooling, but a serious desire to understand. These were people who had little time to read, but who wanted hard information on a range of topics, from immediate trade-union issues to more general political questions. Though its circulation never exceeded two thousand, it exercised a real influence. It built up a team of international correspondents from the syndicalist current around the world, including William Z Foster from the USA and Tom Mann from Britain. Mann, who had spent some years in Australia, wrote of the experience of state arbitration through wages boards or wages councils there. There was a readership outside France; one of the subscribers in Switzerland was Zinoviev, future president of the Comintern, who may well have passed his copy to his neighbour Lenin. When the young Ho Chi Minh arrived in Paris from Indochina in 1919, one of the first places he visited was the *Vie ouvrière* office.

The outbreak of war in 1914 changed everything. It was not only the Second International which collapsed; syndicalists and anarchists flocked to support their own national governments. In France, just days before the declaration of war there had been massive anti-war demonstrations on the streets of Paris.

But then the syndicalist daily paper, *La Bataille syndicaliste*, made a complete turnabout and supported the war. CGT leader Jouhaux worked closely within government institutions during the war.

Alfred Rosmer has left a vivid account of how he and Monatte found themselves totally isolated.[10] They visited individuals whom they had thought to be sympathetic to the politics of *La Vie ouvrière*, only to find they had gone over to support for the war. It was obviously impossible to go on producing the journal. They were reduced to gathering around themselves a small number of individuals. One of these was the writer Marcel Martinet, later to be cultural editor of the Communist daily *L'Humanité*. (In 1919 Martinet's novel about the war would be runner-up to Proust for the prestigious Goncourt prize.[11])

Only in 1915 was Rosmer able to circulate a statement to former subscribers to *La Vie ouvrière*, setting out the bases for an internationalist opposition to the war. He condemned those French Socialists who "make all German workers unanimously responsible for the treachery of some of their leaders".[12]

Meanwhile other significant contacts had been made. Leon Trotsky and some other Russian revolutionaries, including Radek and Lunacharsky, had established an anti-war daily paper in Paris, *Nashe Slovo* (Our Word). They quickly recognised an affinity with the remnants of the *Vie ouvrière* grouping, and a close association developed, which was to have significance for the future.

Some small-scale actions remained possible. In May 1915 Rosmer cooperated with the production of an issue of the paper of the metal workers' union. Strict censorship was in force. An article was included expressing anti-war sentiments, and

---

10. Rosmer 1936, pp209-16.
11. Paizis 2007.
12. Rosmer 1936, p548.

giving information about strikes in Scotland which had not been reported in France. The censors demanded the removal of the offending article. Some copies of the duly censored paper were produced – and a large number of the original version. Piles of the uncensored paper were packed, wrapped in a few copies of the censored version. The authorities were deceived and the subversive article got wide circulation among trade unionists.

But the most important activity was the preparation for the Zimmerwald conference in Switzerland in September 1915. Though involving only a small number, this conference marked the beginning of the reconstruction of an international – and internationalist – labour movement. In France the syndicalists played an important role in building Zimmerwald. In his history of the labour movement during the war Rosmer mocked later Russian accounts which referred to Lenin's role in building in France – as he pointed out, at this time nobody in France had ever heard of Lenin.[13] Rosmer himself played an important role in organising and Merrheim was one of the delegates. Report-back meetings played an important part in building an oppositional current.

There was no right of conscientious objection in France, and in any case syndicalists believed that they should go to the army and suffer the same conditions as their fellow-workers. Pierre Monatte accepted the call-up – but made it clear that he would not load his gun – he said he could not continue to be politically active if he had been responsible for the death of German workers. There was a threat to shoot him, but he became a signaller and was commended for repairing telephone lines under fire.[14]

But it was virtually impossible to do political work under conditions of trench warfare and with a large peasant army. There is no evidence of any syndicalist role during the 1917

13. Rosmer 1936, p461.
14. Monatte 2018.

mutinies, which seem to have been largely spontaneous – though of course individuals may have been touched by anti-militarist propaganda before or during the war. The syndicalists remained a tiny minority – but one whose significance would be shown in the post-war period.

The October Revolution of 1917 changed everything and opened up a new period for the revolutionary movement throughout the world. For millions of working people, even if they had only a vague understanding of what was happening in Russia, it represented a very concrete hope of a new direction for the labour movement, and indeed for the whole of humanity. The old certainties, the old alliances and divisions were called into question.

Historians, whether sympathetic or hostile, rightly lay stress on the role of Lenin and the Bolsheviks in making the revolution. But the Bolsheviks did not make the revolution all on their own; from the very outset they sought, and found, allies. The military committee which organised the October insurrection included four anarchists. One of these was the remarkable Bill Shatov. Of Russian origin, Shatov had lived in the United States and had been a member of the IWW. He went on to play an active part in the defence of the revolution and held various positions of responsibility in the revolutionary regime.

With October the revolution was entering uncharted waters. There was no clear road ahead, merely problems, contradictions and looming threats that could destroy the whole project. Above all the revolution needed allies. Only support from the international working class could counter the immediate military threat; and only the internationalisation of the revolution could ensure the survival of its principles. As Trotsky put it at the Third Congress:

> When another stronghold is erected in France or in Germany, then the one in Russia will lose nine-tenths of its significance; and we

will then stand ready to go to you in Europe in order to defend this other, more important stronghold.[15]

The image of Lenin, among friends and foes, is of a hard man who repeatedly split from those who deviated from the "correct" line. (I used to have on my bookshelves a volume, produced in Moscow, entitled "Lenin Against Conciliationism".) But Lenin knew when to conciliate as well as when to split; if his self-appointed followers have been much better at splitting, it is because it is much easier.

The question became central at the Second Congress of the Comintern in the summer of 1920. Few Communist Parties existed as yet, and a range of organisations and individuals had been invited. These included a number of anarchists and syndicalists from Western Europe. They came, motivated by hope, curiosity, or a mixture of the two. They did not come with the illusions of later visitors, and knew they would find a country ravaged by upheaval and civil war, but wished to see how the new order was being built. Travel to Russia was not easy in the aftermath of the world war.[16]

But the Second Congress was far from unanimous in its welcome to the syndicalist delegates. Paul Levi, leader of the newly founded German Communist Party, had faced opposition in his own party from ultra-lefts who opposed participation in elections and reformist trade unions. His response had been, not to try to win over at least some, but to expel them. Now when the Congress debated the need to build revolutionary parties, he made no attempt to engage with those coming from different traditions:

> It seems to me that clarifying the differences between communism
> on the one hand and the anarchist views of the Spanish comrade
> on the other is quite out of line with the tasks of this congress, nor
> does it serve the interests of what the world today is demanding

15. Riddell 2015, p379.
16. See Mazuy 2002.

of the Communist International, namely, fully defining a course of action. We get no closer to carrying out this task by focusing the discussion on a question that the majority of the Western European working class settled decades ago.[17]

Zinoviev was similarly dismissive. (This debate makes clear that there was no such thing as a single Bolshevik position.) He lectured the delegates on the history of the Bolshevik Party: "Had we not had a centralised party built along military lines, with iron discipline, organized over the course of twenty years, by now we doubtless would have been defeated twenty times over".[18] He omitted to mention that such "iron discipline" had not been seen in 1917, when Zinoviev himself had argued publicly against the insurrection.

Lenin very visibly dissented. Responding to a delegate from the British Shop Stewards' Movement, he argued that "if Comrade Tanner says that he is opposed to parties, but at the same time is in favour of a minority that represents the best organised and most revolutionary workers showing the way to the entire proletariat, then I say that there is really no difference between us".[19] It was a remarkable attempt at a reconciliation between two different traditions.

Trotsky responded equally vigorously, evoking his own experience of working with French syndicalists and insisting that:

> Just because I know that the party is indispensable, and am very well aware of the value of the party, and just because I see Scheidemann on the one side and, on the other, American or Spanish or French syndicalists who not only wish to fight against the bourgeoisie but who, unlike Scheidemann, really want to tear its head off – for this reason I say that I prefer to discuss with these Spanish, American and French comrades in order to prove to them that the party is

---

17. Riddell 1991, Vol. I, p166.
18. Riddell 1991, Vol. I, pp150-51.
19. Lenin 1920.

> indispensable for the fulfillment of the historical mission which is
> placed upon them – the destruction of the bourgeoisie.[20]

If there were conservative and sectarian attitudes within the Comintern, such attitudes were also far from uncommon among the syndicalists. The IWW's response to the Comintern was a self-satisfied assurance that its own traditions and analysis were quite adequate:

> We have no reason to be excited by the invitation. The programme of the IWW was valid before the war, survived the war without the necessity to alter even a single point, it is valid now and will with absolute necessity be the programme of every revolutionary party.[21]

In France Pierre Monatte, though he had supported the Comintern, refused to join the new organisation until 1923, when he could have played a positive role by encouraging other syndicalists to join and ensuring that their distinctive contribution was recognised.

But despite the heated debates, there was a general recognition of the urgency of building the Comintern. If the revolution was to survive, it had to be spread within a few years. That required revolutionary parties throughout Europe and beyond, and every means had to be used. Pierre Broué has shown that the formation of the Comintern was a complex process, in which individuals, networks of personal contacts, the various "foreign sections" based on ex-prisoners-of-war in Russia, small political groups and mass parties all interacted in the context of a unique revolutionary wave.[22]

But central to the strategy was the task of splitting the existing mass organisations of the working class. Throughout Europe the parties of the Second International had backed the war in 1914, with the anti-war minorities being marginalised. But at the end of the war radicalised workers were

20. Trotsky 1920.
21. Tosstorff 2004, p107.
22. Broué 1997.

looking for ways to achieve social change, and often they turned to the traditional organisations of their class, while being impatient with the old leaderships. This offered excellent opportunities for provoking splits and establishing new mass parties.

Yet this process is often invoked and quoted in oversimplified form. Only in a handful of countries were Communist Parties created from splits in mass social-democratic parties. The circumstances were complex and historically unique – scarcely enough to justify arguing that it is a universal principle that revolutionaries should always work inside existing mass reformist parties.

The point can be illustrated from the history of the French Communist Party (PCF). In later years historians, whether Communist or anti-Communist, have been at pains to stress the continuity between the birth of the party and its subsequent Stalinist evolution. Many of those who played a key role in the Party's early years have simply disappeared from the historical record, since they left, or were expelled, before 1930.[23]

In fact a number of syndicalists, notably Rosmer and Monatte, as well as other non-members of the Socialist Party (SFIO), played an important role in the process which led to the split in the party and the foundation of the PCF at Christmas 1920. Political lines were drawn loosely at the time, and non-members used to participate in SFIO meetings.[24]

Alfred Rosmer was not present at the founding congress of the PCF, but his wife-to-be, Marguerite Thévenet, played an important role. Clara Zetkin, who entered France illegally to address the congress, wrote personally to Lenin to give her impressions and stressed that Madame Rosmer was "one of the most lucid, loyal, energetic and politically intelligent 'men' in the French movement".[25]

---

23. Birchall 2011.
24. Ferrette 2011.
25. Zetkin 1921.

In the early years syndicalists played a major role. After returning from Moscow Rosmer briefly played a leading role in the French Communist Party. When Monatte finally joined in 1923 he rapidly became a member of the Central Committee. Robert Louzon, living in Tunisia, helped to launch the first Arabic-language Communist daily paper – promptly suppressed by the authorities. Marcel Martinet became an imaginative cultural editor of *L'Humanité*. Trotsky recalled that at one point in the early twenties Lenin had said to him that the leadership of the PCF should be removed and replaced by the *Vie ouvrière* team.[26] (Of course at that stage Moscow did not have the power to intervene in this fashion.)

One initiative taken by the Second Comintern Congress was the decision to found the Red International of Labour Unions (RILU or Profintern). Syndicalists were organised in trade unions, not in parties, and unions could not affiliate to the Comintern. So it was proposed to establish an international body, parallel to the Comintern, which trade unions could join. It was stressed that this was not an attempt to split existing unions, and that Communists should strive to remain in the existing unions even when attempts were made to expel them.

Historians, even those sympathetic to the Comintern, have tended to take a negative view of the RILU. Tony Cliff and Donny Gluckstein as well as Ralph Darlington have described it in very uncomplimentary terms.[27]

But if the whole RILU project was open to criticism, it is hard to see what alternative there was. Zinoviev's proposal that unions should affiliate to the Comintern alongside parties was impracticable. The Comintern needed a way to relate to the syndicalists, and it needed it quickly.

The international body organising the existing trade

---

26. Cited in Paizis 2007, p211.
27. Cliff and Gluckstein 1986, Darlington 2008; see also Tosstorff 2004.

unions was the solidly reformist International Federation of Trade Unions (IFTU), known as the Amsterdam International. But if the Comintern was right to attack its reformist leadership, claims of its impending demise were much exaggerated. Thus in 1921 the Comintern predicted the "imminent and complete collapse" of the IFTU.[28] In fact the IFTU would survive longer than the RILU.

The person put in charge of organising the RILU's founding congress was Alfred Rosmer. There could have been no better choice. He had come out of the syndicalist tradition, and appreciated both its strengths and its weaknesses. As a journalist for *La Vie ouvrière* he had reported on countries from Britain to South Africa, and had a good knowledge of the international labour movement.

Unfortunately, Zinoviev, with whom he had to work, did not share these qualities. Zinoviev thought it enough to denounce reformist leaders, believing workers would be convinced by having their leaders insulted. Thus an "appeal" to the IFTU began: "You are the chief bulwark of capitalism, now living out its last days – you are the watchdogs of capital, barking furiously at all those who approach your master's lair".[29] It was a sign of the shortage of competent and experienced cadre that the new Russian state had to give so many senior responsibilities to a mediocrity like Zinoviev.

The founding congress of the RILU was held in the summer of 1921, at the time of the Third Congress of the Comintern; it was attended by 380 delegates. It was not a carefully stage-managed event. At one point uproar broke out when syndicalist delegates raised the question of the position of anarchists in Russia:

> Delegates stood on their chairs and sang the *Internationale* when Lozovsky tried to speak. For several minutes the meeting hall

---

28. Riddell 2015, p62.
29. Degras 1971, pp204-5.

> was rather like the New York Stock Exchange. Everybody was shouting, including the spectators, who left their seats to invade the conference area.[30]

But this was just an example of the friction that was inevitable when two different traditions came together and attempted to cooperate.

Much debate centred on the sterile question of the formal relation between the RILU and the Comintern, with the syndicalists being very suspicious of any suggestion that they were being subordinated to a "political" organisation. In the longer term the results were distinctly meagre, with the RILU being given a very minor place in Comintern strategy, before it was finally wound up in 1937.

In any case things were changing rapidly from the end of 1922 onwards. Lenin was effectively incapacitated after his last speech to the Comintern in November. He had warned of the dangers of imposing the Russian experience on the international movement, and urged thought and study, warning that "we have not learnt how to present our Russian experience to foreigners".[31] He was cheered to the rafters, but it seemed nobody was actually listening. Zinoviev was now free to try to shape the Comintern; he prepared the way for Stalin and his own eradication.

A policy of "bolshevisation" was now applied to the parties of the Comintern. Essentially this meant tighter control from Moscow and what Rosmer called "mechanical and slavish imitation of Russian methods".[32]

Many of the most thoughtful and imaginative individuals who had come to the Comintern in 1920, including most of those from a syndicalist background, became disenchanted and over the next few years most of them left or were expelled. They were replaced by others who were prepared to accept total

---

30. Tosstorff 2004, p348.
31. Lenin 1922.
32. Rosmer 2016, p219.

subordination to Moscow. As Pierre Broué put it, by 1924 the Comintern had "a single, centralised and disciplined apparatus of professional militants, reproduced on the model of the Soviet party, led from Moscow and in conformity with Soviet foreign policy".[33]

In France the leading figures of syndicalist origin, Rosmer and Monatte, were expelled in 1924, because they had argued that the newly elected British Labour government should be responded to by a careful application of the united front strategy rather than with simple denunciations.

We should be very cautious about trying to draw lessons from the Comintern experience. Today's world is very different from that of October 1917, and history will not repeat itself. In 1968, when a worldwide upturn in struggle seemed to put revolutionary change on the agenda again, many of us recognised the need for organisation – and since Leninism and the Comintern were the only precedents we had, we used them as models. But it is now time to take a more sceptical attitude to that heritage.

One of the roots of the terrible sectarianism which has blighted the far left is the belief that a single political tradition embodies the sole truth. As Peter Sedgwick put it, too many socialists try to establish "an Apostolic succession from the ideas of certain revered forerunners to those of their (usually self-enthroned) successors in the present day".[34] The Comintern experience seems to suggest that Tony Cliff was nearer the truth when he argued that "ideas are like a river and a river is formed from lots of streams".[35] The aftermath of 1917 saw followers of different traditions come together to defend and emulate the Russian Revolution. At best they could have complemented and enriched each other – just as Victor Serge

---

33. Broué 1997, pp384-5.
34. Sedgwick 1960.
35. Cliff 1996.

argued that the anarchist preoccupation with morality could provide a valuable counterbalance to Marxism.[36]

Sadly this often did not happen. In the early 1920s, when Mussolini was rising to prominence, a mass anti-fascist movement, the *Arditi del Popolo*, grew up independently of the Italian Communist Party; the Communists regarded it with scorn, and failed to work with it, let alone learn from its experience.[37]

Likewise, when Trotsky was drawing together the Fourth International, he was deeply suspicious of any political currents independent of the orthodoxy he had defined. That militants of the quality of Victor Serge and Alfred and Marguerite Rosmer found themselves outside the Fourth International from the beginning was a clear indication of the weakness of an organisation condemned to repeated splits, with each fragment claiming to be the sole possessor of truth.

In more recent years the Marxist left has encountered alternative currents. Just as syndicalism grew up in reaction to the corruption and pettiness of parliamentary politics, so too the anti-capitalist movement of the early twenty-first century was contemptuous of orthodox politics and Marxists had to look for common ground for joint action. Likewise Extinction Rebellion and other climate groups have developed new styles of activism; if Marxists can contribute important insights to the struggle against climate change, they need to recognise what can be learned from new organisations and movements. History does not repeat itself, but by studying how socialists in the past confronted unprecedented situations, we can prepare ourselves for the unforeseen circumstances that lie ahead of us.

---

36. Serge 2011.
37. Behan 2003.

References

Allen, Barbara C 2016, *Alexander Shlyapnikov 1885-1937: Life of an Old Bolshevik*, Haymarket.

Behan, Tom 2003, *The Resistible Rise of Benito Mussolini*, Bookmarks.

Birchall, Ian 2011, "PCF: The Missing Founders", http://grimanddim.org/historical-writings/2011-pcf-the-missing-founders/.

Broué, Pierre, 1997, *Histoire de l'Internationale Communiste*, Fayard.

Charter of Amiens 1906, https://www.marxists.org/history/france/cgt/charter-amiens.htm.

Chuzeville, Julien 2017, *Un Court Moment Révolutionnaire: La création du parti communiste en France (1915-1924)*, Libertalia.

Cliff, Tony 1996, "Engels", https://www.marxists.org/archive/cliff/works/1996/07/engels.htm.

Cliff, Tony and Donny Gluckstein 1986, *Marxism and Trade Union Struggle: The General Strike of 1926*, Bookmarks.

Cyr, Frédéric 2013, *Paul Levi, rebelle devant les extrêmes*, Presses de l'Université Laval.

Darlington, Ralph 2008, *Syndicalism and the Transition to Communism*, Ashgate.

Degras, Jane (ed.) 1971, *The Communist International 1919-1943*, Volume I, Frank Cass.

Dubief, Henri 1969, *Le Syndicalisme Révolutionnaire*, Armand Colin.

Ferrette, François 2011, *La Véritable Histoire du Parti Communiste Français*, Éditions Demopolis.

Fernbach, David (ed.) 2011, *In the Steps of Rosa Luxemburg: Selected writings of Paul Levi*, Brill.

Frölich, Paul 2013, *Im radikalen Lager: Politische Autobiographie 1890-1921* (ed. Reiner Tosstorff), BasisDruck Verlag.

Lenin, VI 1920, Speech to Second Congress, https://www.marxists.org/archive/lenin/works/1920/jul/x03.htm#fw2.

Lenin, VI 1922, Speech to the Fourth Congress of the Communist International, https://www.marxists.org/archive/lenin/works/1922/nov/04b.htm.

Mazuy, Rachel 2002, *Croire plutôt que voir? Voyages en Russie soviétique (1919-1939)*, Odile Jacob.

Merrheim, Alphonse 1911, "L'Approche de la guerre", *La Vie ouvrière*, 5 and 20 January, 5 and 20 February.

Monatte, Pierre 2018, *Lettres d'un syndicaliste sous l'uniforme 1915-1918* (ed. Julien Chuzeville), Smolny.

Paizis, George 2007, *Marcel Martinet: Poet of the revolution*, Francis Boutle.

Riddell, John (ed.) 1987, *Founding the Communist International: Proceedings and documents of the First Congress*, March 1919, Pathfinder.

Riddell, John (ed.) 1991, *Workers of the World and Oppressed Peoples, Unite! Proceedings and documents of the Second Congress, 1920*, two volumes, Pathfinder.

Riddell, John (ed.) 2011, *Toward the United Front: Proceedings of the Fourth Congress of the Communist International, 1922*, Brill.

Riddell, John (ed.) 2015, *To The Masses: Proceedings of the Third Congress of the Communist International, 1921*, Brill.

Rosmer, Alfred 2016, *Lenin's Moscow*, Haymarket.

Rosmer, Alfred 1921, Speech to the Congress of the Red International of Labour Unions in July 1921, *Revolutionary History*, Vol. 7, No 4, Winter 2000-2001.

Rosmer, Alfred 1936, *Le Mouvement ouvrier pendant la guerre*, Volume I, Librairie du travail.

Sedgwick, Peter 1960, "The Fight for Workers' Control", *International Socialism*, 3, Winter 1960-61, https://www.marxists.org/archive/sedgwick/1960/xx/workerscontrol.htm.

Serge, Victor 2011, "The Anarchists and the Experience of the Russian Revolution" in *Revolution in Danger*, Haymarket.

Tosstorff, Reiner 2004, *Profintern: Die Rote Gewerkschaftsinternationale 1920–1937*, Ferdinand Schoeningh.

Trotsky, Leon 1920, Speech to the Second Congress of the Communist International, https://www.marxists.org/archive/trotsky/1924/ffyci-1/ch11.htm.

Zetkin, Clara 1921, Letter of 25 January in R Stoljarowa & P Schmalfuss (eds), *Briefe Deutscher an Lenin 1917-1923* Dietz Verlag, 1990.

Further reading

Alfred Rosmer, Lenin's Moscow, *Haymarket, 2016.*
Remains an invaluable source as a participant account.

Ralph Darlington, Syndicalism and the Transition to Communism, *Ashgate, 2008.*
An excellent international survey of syndicalism before and after 1914.

Reiner Tosstorff, The Red International of Labour Unions (RILU) 1920–1937, *Haymarket, 2018.*
A very full, detailed account of the RILU.

Robert Wohl, French Communism in the Making, 1914-1924, *Stanford UP, 1966.*
Now very old, but still one of the best things in English on the origins of French Communism, using interviews with participants and independent of French political alignments.

APRIL HOLCOMBE

The freedom to be: Marxism, gender oppression and the struggle for trans liberation

> **April Holcombe** is a transgender woman and contributor to *Red Flag* newspaper. She was a leading activist in the successful campaign for marriage equality. In non-pandemic times, she teaches English as a Foreign Language.

An extended review of Laura Miles, Transgender Resistance: Socialism and the fight for trans liberation, *Bookmarks 2020.*

TRANSGENDER PEOPLE ARE in a paradoxical situation internationally. The world has never had so many visible trans people in popular culture, the media and even now in politics. Broadly speaking, public attitudes have shifted quite quickly in favour of trans people, although this is mixed. An Australian survey of 54,000 people last year found that 45 percent agree there are more than two genders, and just 38 percent disagree.[1]

On the other hand, trans people have become a favoured punching bag of right-wing politicians. In the midst of a global pandemic, having just acquired effectively dictatorial powers, Hungarian prime minister Viktor Orbán is putting legislation to define gender as "biological sex based on primary sex characteristics and chromosomes" and thus make it impossible for people to legally change their gender.[2] One-third of Poland is under the control of councils that have declared their jurisdictions "LGBT-free zones".[3] In the United States, Trump

1. Hanrahan 2019.
2. Walker 2020.
3. Ciobanu 2020.

is planning to roll back provisions protecting LGBTI people from discrimination in healthcare and health insurance and Australian prime minister Scott Morrison has a very similar attack proposed with the Religious Freedom Bill.[4]

Most importantly, the statistics still show trans lives scarred by violence, poverty and despair. In countries like the USA and Australia, trans people are twice as likely to be unemployed, four times as likely to experience sexual violence, and 40 percent report having attempted suicide.[5]

Laura Miles' *Transgender Resistance* is a valuable and timely contribution at a time of flux, danger, hope and controversy in trans lives. The book acts as a compendium of transgender history, science, theory and politics. As Miles discusses these aspects of trans experience in turn, she both applies, and argues for, a revolutionary Marxist method. As such, *Transgender Resistance* will benefit transgender people new to Marxism, as well as Marxists new to transgender politics.

In this article, I hope to summarise each of these aspects in turn. In doing so, I have sometimes contributed some of my own ideas in support of Miles' arguments – in particular on questions raised around gender socialisation, self-identification, and identity politics. I believe these additions to be consistent with Miles' framework.

Gender history

While contemporary trans identity is shaped by the circumstances in which it has arisen, trans people are not a purely novel product of modernity or postmodernity. Gender variance stretches back as far as gender itself. Before the emergence of classes, societies were characterised by cooperative ways of living and cultures that valued equality. Pregnancy, childbirth and breastfeeding created practical distinctions between men and women and some of the work they did. Yet this

---

4. Holcombe 2019.
5. James et al 2015; Callander et al 2019.

differentiation did not exist to oppress: individual preferences were not only accepted, but often accounted for with distinct genders.

The anthropological record of early societies is rich with traditions beyond the gender binary. Miles provides us with a sample of these practices, drawing from Leslie Feinberg's extensive discussion in *Transgender Warriors* (1996) and sexologist Magnus Hirschfeld's radical study *Transvestites* (1910). The most notable case is the gender diversity found in practically every Native American tribe before European colonisation. Documented encounters between early Jesuits and indigenous people show that gender variation was widespread and accepted, and that the colonisers detested this. The French Jesuit Joseph-François Lafitau, who spent six years among the Iroquois, reported seeing "women with manly courage who prided themselves upon the profession of warrior" and "men cowardly enough to live as women".[6] The most well-documented phenomenon is the "Two Spirit" or "bade" person. These were typically boys who transitioned to womanhood, and thereafter dressed and worked as women, and took male sexual partners. Similar roles are well documented as far afield as sub-Saharan Africa, Siberia, Southeast Asia, and the Pacific Islands. The Bugis people of Indonesia still practise five distinct gender roles.

The "third gender" often performed a religious and/or medicinal role in society. Intersexuality is a dominant theme amongst early religions. Divine beings frequently possessed both male and female anatomy, examples of which remained in the mythologies of ancient Sumer, Egypt, Greece, China and India. "Mother Earth" herself was more likely a being of indeterminate sex representing the time before humanity divided into male and female. "The experience of being a Two-Spirit person – one whose gender status was different from both men and women – was thought to confer a capacity for wisdom and

---

6. Miles 2020, p23.

greater understanding of the human condition."[7] Although attitudes differed from society to society, and Miles cautions us against overly romanticising some cultural practices, the evidence clearly demonstrates that early societies held much more flexible and egalitarian views on gender – even where men and women's roles did differ, they were seen as equally essential contributions to society.[8]

Gender oppression

The historical record demonstrates that women's oppression, homophobia and transphobia have not existed in all societies. These are not natural phenomena rooted in biology, but social phenomena that can be abolished if the conditions that gave rise to them are also abolished. Miles draws on Friedrich Engels' work to explain how gender oppression is rooted in societal changes. In *The Origins of the Family, Private Property and the State*, Engels explains how women were subjugated through the historical process of societies settling, and then dividing into classes. With the development of agriculture, many more children were possible than in hunter-gatherer societies, so women were more frequently precluded from heavy labour in the fields. While work performed by women remained essential, their subsistence became increasingly dependent on work performed by men. It was through the ploughing of the land and the raising of livestock that wealth could be accumulated, owned and passed on. This property became inherited by the son from his father, which meant establishing paternity was necessary for the correct transfer of property. Patrilineality (kinship derived through the father's lineage) supplanted the ancient and more obvious means of ascertaining family ties through the mother (matrilineality). This was a very protracted process that Engels characterised as the "world-historic defeat

---

7. Miles 2020, p23.
8. For a more detailed investigation of early society's cultural practices around gender, see Feinberg 1996.

of the female sex". "All the surplus which the acquisitions of the necessities of life now yielded fell to the man", Engels wrote in 1884, "the woman shared in its enjoyment, but had no part in its ownership".[9]

The crucial factor, however, was the way that inherited property and settled agriculture allowed for the accretion of unequal wealth between producers over successive generations. As wealth concentrated not just under the ownership of men, but an organised *minority* of men who used it to control the labour of society, women's status was decisively devalued to that of a mere vessel for producing heirs on one side, and the incubator of labourers on the other.

As divisions deepened between men and women's roles, so too did proscriptions against homosexual acts and cross-dressing. The strict sexual codes of the Old Testament show how some of the first class societies sought to enforce the patriarchal family structure against customs and traditions that would have lingered on from earlier times. Such codes were also directed at destroying the local culture and authority of rival societies they conquered, as Miles suggests is the real story behind Sodom and Gomorrah.[10] As class societies grew and dominated, they cemented women's oppression and sexual repression so deeply into the fabric of life that gender oppression can now appear as old as humanity itself.

Oppression has differed in precise character from one class society to another. Capitalist gender ideology – the gender binary, the inferiority of women, "natural" reproductive roles – is built on the material foundations of the nuclear family, which itself emerged from the crisis facing early industrial capitalism. In nineteenth century Britain, rapid industrialisation had torn the peasant family apart and driven its members off the land into filthy urban centres. Men, women and children were thrown together into factories and barrack-like accommodation.

---

9. Engels 1902 (1884), p220.
10. Miles 2020, p27.

The industrial revolution led to untold misery: in 1845, the life expectancy in Manchester for a working-class person was 17. This crisis of mortality threatened the supply of labour, and the turbulence and dysfunction of urban life threatened labour discipline.

Legislation against child labour and for shorter working hours was passed from the 1840s to the 1860s. The new family wage was ostensibly to cover the male worker, his wife and all dependents. Women were supposed to stay at home, raise children and perform unpaid domestic work. Children would learn discipline from their parents and conformity from school. As Miles explains, the bourgeoisie had a ready model to impose on workers' private lives that accorded with their goal of social stability:

> Much of the legislation was about attempting to mould the working class family in the image of the bourgeois family to enable the capitalist class to exert the greater control of the working class through encouraging identification with middle class values of morality – "family values", the Church, temperance, and the discouragement of sex outside marriage.[11]

The nuclear family did not come naturally. Unlike the patriarchal peasant household, which bound its members to each other and the soil, the anonymity of urban life provided opportunities to form relations and communities in a variety of ways. Capitalism was "in practice creating the conditions for the emergence of freer sexual relationships and gender roles among working class people".[12] Women would often dress themselves as men, to access better jobs and pay, or to form covert relationships with other women. Molly houses, where working-class men would go to cross-dress and form sexual relationships, proliferated across the country, but were frequently raided by police and Puritan mobs.

---

11. Miles 2020, p30.
12. Miles 2020, p28.

Establishing discipline meant using the state to criminalise such sexual "deviants". In 1860, the British empire introduced Section 377 of the Indian Penal Code, which applied to all British colonies across Asia, Africa and the Pacific. This outlawed all sexual acts "against the order of nature" as well as third gender groups such as the Indian *hijra*. Domestic laws against sodomy were strengthened in 1885, which infamously put Oscar Wilde behind bars in 1895.

Gender science

Fundamentally, ideological attacks on trans people rest on the belief that men, women and their differences are biological facts for all time and all people. "Biological isn't bigotry", opponents say. Yet, as Miles astutely notes, the biological sciences have been a central ideological prop in justifying the inequality and oppression of capitalism since the nineteenth century. Bourgeois sexual morality was refracted through medical and scientific fields already obsessed with questions of moral hygiene and racial fitness. Female sexuality, homosexuality and masturbation were deemed pathological afflictions or inborn abnormalities. Sexual behaviour was not proscribed in one heap, as in feudal repression of "sodomy", but categorised, catalogued and classified. Capitalism sought a more rationalist ideological condemnation, which "science" provided. "Gender dysphoria" is still listed in the *Diagnostic and Statistical Manual of Mental Disorders*, the handbook of psychiatrists.

Miles employs a wealth of scientific research to demonstrate the complexities of sex. In reality, biological sex is not a clear-cut binary, but a spectrum with many chromosomal, hormonal and physical variations. The same is true for our brains, with studies finding very weak differences between the sexes, and these do not account for the effect of a lifetime of gender-conditioning on our brains, or hormonal treatment in the case of trans subjects. This means we should reject the explanation that trans men, for example, have a "male brain" in a female body. This argument, understandably, is sometimes raised by trans people defending their existence. But if most men don't have a male brain, it begs the question why trans men ought to. Arguments for trans liberation must critique the very assumption that gender difference is a biological fact. The fact that gender is assigned based on genitalia gives the illusion that all differences between men and women stem from their biology. Gender identity is instead a complex interplay of "the person's self-perceived body, their biological sex, the social perception of their body in the eyes of others, social factors like gender values and expectations, and…their sexuality".[13] Gender encompasses so much more than biological sex that socialists should confidently argue that trans women are women, and trans men are men, despite not conforming biologically. Self-identification is a sufficient means of determining one's gender. Trans people's challenge to biological determinism has also opened the space for people to affirm nonbinary gender identities (neither male nor female) – in which no underlying biological assumptions exist at all.

Gender politics

After World War I, the situation for gender-variant people advanced in Weimar Germany and revolutionary Russia, until the workers' movement was crushed by Nazism and Stalinism respectively. Between the horrors of the 1930s and conservatism of the 1950s, history arguably reached its lowest point with regard to sexual liberation. This was truly a dark age for LGBTI people.

Things decisively shifted with the Stonewall riots of 1969. Gay communities had been growing in New York, Los Angeles and San Francisco ever since US soldiers arrived at their ports after World War II. From the mid-1950s to early 60s, activism was predicated on the conservative approach of politely picketing the White House and wearing suits and dresses to

13. Miles 2020, p53.

demonstrate that "homophiles" were just like heterosexuals. But the influence of the Black Power and anti-war movements radicalised the gay ghetto, especially young and gender-non-conforming members of the community. Since repression was so severe, a broad spectrum of behaviour and identities were outcast together, and lines of demarcation between gay and trans, though discernible, were less clear than today. Homosexuals who did not transgress gender stereotypes were still forced to live their lives secretly, but those whose gender expression violated norms were the most marginalised. Resentment at constant police harassment and brutality bubbled under the surface throughout the 1960s, occasionally breaking over. In 1966, a riot broke out at Compton's Cafeteria in San Francisco, when a trans woman threw her coffee in the face of a police officer attempting to arrest her.

Stonewall – also sparked by relentless police harassment – was a turning point because of the depth of anger, the mass nature of the three days of rioting, and its rapid politicisation with the formation of the anti-capitalist Gay Liberation Front.[14] Dick Leitsch, a leading GLF activist and riot participant, noted how at the forefront of the rioting were the trans women and effeminate gay men who constituted the most oppressed underclass of the community.

> The most striking feature of the rioting was that it was led by "queens", not "homosexuals". Homosexuals had been sitting back and taking whatever the establishment handed out; the queens were having none of that...they scored the points and proved that they were not going to tolerate any more harassment and abuse... their bravery and daring saved many people from being hurt.[15]

Miles helpfully contributes to restoring trans people to this period of Gay Liberation struggle. The front cover of

---

14. For a definitive social history of Stonewall and its aftermath, see Carter 2004. Vale to the author who passed away in May 2020.
15. Quoted in Miles 2020, p98.

Transgender Resistance is a photograph of Marsha P Johnson and Sylvia Rivera – two trans women, and radical leaders in the Stonewall riots and Gay Liberation.

However, as early as 1972, movements were fracturing and lowering their sights from liberation to reforming capitalism. While rights for homosexuals could be argued for on the basis that "what people do in the bedroom is their own business", gender nonconformity is public and visible. A turn to moderation therefore included disinterest or even hostility to gender presentation that was too confronting – not just transgender people, but any gays who would "flaunt" it too brazenly. At the 1974 Pride parade, Rivera was booed off the stage by rally participants. Trans and gay struggles did not entirely break and drew somewhat closer together in the 1990s when the acronym LGBT was coined. But whereas homosexuality is accepted by the majority of many Western countries, trans is uneasily balanced between being accepted under the same logic, and being rejected as a step too far.

Trans people's existence pulls at deeply rooted ideas about gender, and both the traditional right and the new far right are determined to safeguard traditional gender roles and the nuclear family. Culture wars against transgender people, and especially transgender youth, are taking place almost everywhere. In chapters 6, 7 and 8, Miles documents these attacks and the situation broadly for transgender people in almost every region in the world, with particular focus on the United States and the United Kingdom. These chapters are a useful resource on the concrete situation, including reforms that have been won through the tireless work of activists. However, the country by country breakdown and detailed legal histories is a little heavy on empirical information and light on analysis. At times, the book feels overloaded with quotes, sources and raw data.

Gender theory

The situation with the Gender Recognition Act (GRA) in Britain earns special attention because of the deplorable role played by feminist organisations like Woman's Place UK. The GRA was passed in 2004 and allows transgender people to change the sex on their birth certificate. Applicants must have lived for two years in their affirmed gender and a psychiatric diagnosis of "gender dysphoria" is required. In 2017, a proposed amendment to simplify this process sparked vocal opposition from the usual conservative voices, but also from groups of feminists, and even some on the left. A bigoted cartoon published in the *Morning Star* in February depicted trans people as lecherous crocodiles, demonstrating the reactionary direction in which "trans-criticism" is taking its advocates.[16]

Unlike our conservative opponents, "trans-critical" feminists centre the issue of women's oppression in their attacks. Their main target is therefore trans women, who they argue are really men. According to Woman's Place UK, women-only services should exclude trans women, to save numbers for "real" women and to prevent male rapists from invading women's spaces. This is a bankrupt argument in many ways. Prioritising cis women (women assigned female at birth) simply means accepting the disgraceful state of funding for women's refuges, health clinics, etc, after a decade of devastating austerity. These are also services that transgender people are in desperate need of. The obvious argument is to demand expanded funding and services for all women – and indeed all people – a stance which encourages solidarity between oppressed communities. But because its exclusionary logic rests on the fact of women's vulnerability as an oppressed group, trans-critical feminism is undermined if it acknowledges that trans people are victims of oppression – including women's oppression – and not

---

16. Milton 2020.

perpetrators. Throughout her polemic, Miles consistently presses the need to forge unity of the oppressed: trans people and women are oppressed by the same system of capitalism and should fight alongside each other to resist sexism, transphobia and homophobia.

This ostensibly left-wing current has also joined in the moral panic over the "epidemic" of young people identifying as transgender, and in many cases beginning the early stages of medical transition. It is tremendously positive that so many people feel not only free to be themselves, but confident to demand the services that will help them get there. On such an issue, it is difficult to see where the feminist argument differs from the conservative one at all. Radical feminists say that the "trans lobby" has infiltrated schools and convinced tomboyish girls that they are really boys. Australian prime minister Scott Morrison also decries the existence of "gender whisperers" in the classroom. The UK's Tory Minister for Women and Equalities announced in April 2020 that central to their revisions to the Gender Recognition Act would be "the protection of single-sex spaces" and preventing young people's access to medical transition.[17] On 14 June, *The Sunday Times* reported that Boris Johnson's government had completely scrapped all plans for progressive GRA reform. "Instead they plan to announce a ban on 'gay-cure' therapies in an attempt to placate LGBT people. New protections will be offered to safeguard female-only spaces, including refuges and public lavatories, to stop them being used by those with male anatomy."[18] This is very obviously a setback for gender liberation, the bitter fruit of a right-wing culture war that enjoys the support of a small number of "radical" cheerleaders.

The claim that trans women are male invaders is both offensive to trans women, and actually reinforces women's oppression more broadly by resting on the idea that women's

17. Truss 2020.
18. Shipman 2020.

oppression stems from somewhere in men's biology. "The prevalence of the belief that trans women pose a threat reflects a common strand in some feminist ideology – the essentialist myth of the inherent non-violent nature of women and the inherent violence of men."[19] This strand of feminist hostility to trans people on a biological basis goes back decades. In her 1979 book *Transsexual Empire: The making of the she-male*, Janice Raymond wrote:

> All transsexuals rape women's bodies by reducing the real female form to an artefact, appropriating this body for themselves... Transsexuals merely cut off the most obvious means of invading women, so that they seem non-invasive.

This extreme hostility might be drawn from theories of patriarchy, but it also stinks of run-of-the-mill bourgeois prejudice.

The trans-critical alternative to crude essentialism is the argument that trans women are men and trans men are women because they were socialised from birth into those roles. However, since gender assignment at birth depends on genitalia, the argument that all women share a common socialisation from birth brings us to identical conclusions to biological determinism. Socialisation is of crucial importance to the foundation of our identities, but it is multifaceted and subject to many contingent factors, especially one's class and nationality. How can the socialisation of a refugee girl and a princess be compared? Broad similarities make women's oppression a coherent and universal phenomenon, but not a uniform one. Just as importantly, transphobia and the deep distress produced by socialisation at odds with one's gender identity clearly also affects the experience of "gendering". Do two boys enjoy the same "privilege" of male socialisation if one is abused by their adult men, bullied at school, and psychologically tormented because of their feminine tendencies?

19. Miles 2020, p200.

Helpfully, Miles also argues against adopting too mechanical a view of how socialisation works:

> If we take the view that gender identity is entirely caused via social construction, then we should not be surprised if those who advocate transgender "cures" conclude that they can eradicate trans people's gender behaviour by "training" them...to behave differently.[20]

If individuals were mechanically determined by socialisation, there would be no way to resist gender oppression at all. But homosexuality, trans identity, women resisting sexism, into which no one is socialised, all prove that neither biology nor socialisation can entirely define our behaviour or identity.

I would articulate an approach to these thorny questions in the following way. Humans are naturally various and capitalism is inherently contradictory. Socialisation cannot iron out such complexity from the psyche of its subjects. For various reasons, individuals reject or rebel against aspects of their socialisation, and assert their humanity by making choices to be who they wish to be, in the face of sexism, homophobia and transphobia. Human agency is a factor in the construction of the self that allows us to reflect, feel, and make choices that go against what is permissible for capitalism.

In this complex mix, socialists should approach gender in its contradiction. The nuclear family is a capitalist institution designed to regulate the private lives of workers, acquire invaluable quantities of unpaid labour from women's domestic labour, invoke labour discipline and ensure a healthy supply of labour for the future of capital accumulation. Gender is the ideological expression of the inequality between men and women reinforced through the cycle of capitalist exploitation and privatised reproduction.

But gender is a central pillar of understanding oneself, a prism through which personality is refracted. Confining

---

20. Miles 2020, p49.

people to one or the other gender is a form of oppression whose devastating impact on those who do not conform is obvious. Self-identification does not undo gender, but it does challenge its supposedly natural origins and weakens its ability to discipline us into acting a certain way. If socialisation helps to produce the self, the self nonetheless has the agency to challenge oppressive conditioning. Championing the ability to self-determine one's gender puts socialists on the side of an oppressed minority, but it also helps to illuminate some of the potential for a society liberated from gender oppression altogether.

Gender strategy

The final section of the book deals with the debates between identity politics and Marxism on the strategies for trans liberation. In this section, I have used different examples from those given by Miles, with the same goal of demonstrating the self-defeating approach of identity politics to oppression and struggle.

The roots of identity politics lie in the postmodern rejection of Marxism that accompanied the decline of working-class struggle in the West in the 1970s. The social movements turned away from class struggle as a leverage of power and looked to new forms of living, changing language and ideas, or reforming the legal and political systems. Postmodernism was an eclectic mix of these impulses, locating the source of power not in the structures of capitalism, but in relations between individuals enmeshed in various interlocking systems of oppression.

Identity politics is predicated on the myriad divisions this produces. Separate struggles must be waged by those who experience each oppression. But trans liberation will be impossible if the struggle is limited to the small minority of trans people. Support from the majority can and must be fought for and won, because of the universal interests of workers that cross the divides of gender, sexuality, race, nationality and so on.

More leftish variants of identity politics, like queer theory and intersectionality, can point out the nuances of interlocking systems of oppression, but they cannot explain why gender oppression actually exists. Queer theory rightly critiques the Pink Dollar – the commercialisation of gay cultural life – and the shift to the neoliberal centre by many gay organisations, but its political strategies are far less clear and far less effective. Laura Miles quotes the poststructuralist Surya Munro, who argues for the "destabilization and subversion of existing categories":

> Drag and cross-dressing [are] queer and challenge heteropatriarchal norms because they expose the ways in which gender is constructed. Thus gender identities are enacted with the aim of destabilising the normalisation of certain types of gender and sexuality, so that we are made aware of how all genders and sexualities are fictitious.[21]

In this approach, fighting gender oppression is something we do as individuals with our behaviour, by not conforming to gender stereotypes, identifying outside the gender binary, or through drag, polyamory (non-monogamy), and so on. Deliberately dressing and acting in nonconforming ways – "gender-fucking" – is good fun, but it does not even begin to touch the material structures that make gender such a persistent reality. Wage labour makes the worker propertyless and dependent on stable employment to feed themselves and their children (as well as elderly, sick and disabled relatives). The division of labour within that nuclear family, and in the paid work that sustains it, reinforces daily the division of man and woman. For billions of people, there are no other economically viable arrangements to raise their children except in a nuclear family, and overwhelmingly the burden of private, unpaid labour falls on women. Alternative forms of childrearing and relationships are sadly not an option.

21. Munro 2005, quoted in Miles 2020, p216.

Identity politics fails to appreciate these material foundations of ideas about gender, because it rejects class as the fundamental division of society. Instead, oppressions are a web of crisscrossing power imbalances; analysis does not take us down to the roots, but round and round the surface appearance. Without a systemic critique of capitalism, individuals' prejudices seem as likely a culprit as any for the oppression trans people face.

"Raising awareness" of the fictitious foundations of gender is only a reformulation of the run-of-the-mill liberal argument that "education is the cure". Confronting the capitalist class is rejected in favour of changing the words and symbols we use, the ways of thinking or the "discourse" through which we understand gender. The aim is not to convince the working class that oppression undermines their collective strength, but to remonstrate with every less-than-perfect understanding of gender. This can and does lead to a middle-class purism that turns inward to an inner circle of those "in the know", the formation of ineffectual silos of "wokeness".

Examples from social movements make this clear. When protesters call restrictions on abortion an attack on women's rights, some queer activists roundly denounce them for implying that only women can become pregnant – when trans men and nonbinary people are also capable. It does not hurt the movement to mention this, but fighting against the use of "women" as an accurate shorthand for the vast majority affected by attacks on abortion turns the movement into a battle of moral superiority among its participants. It sidelines important questions of strategy and tactics that should guide the movement's activities, and brings front and centre a marginal issue of language use whose correction will have no tangible effect on the strength or success of the movement. A strong, mass and united movement would win greater abortion rights, improve life for women and trans men, increase the confidence of the oppressed, and open our minds to other questions of gender oppression. But the obsession with ideological purity from the outset sabotages the potential for ideas to develop in struggle, because the struggle is divided between those "in the know" and the unenlightened "normies" who – however hard they try – are part of the problem.

A similar argument emerged following the Women's March after the inauguration of Donald Trump in January 2017. With four million participants, this was the largest protest in United States history. Many protesters wore pink "pussy" hats in response to Trump's despicable remarks that he can sexually assault any woman he likes because he is a powerful man. The pussy hats received strident criticism from some queer activists for implying that all women have vulvas, or all those with vulvas are women. A professor of gender studies at a Michigan university attacked the hats as "dangerous for trans people". "A lot of the reasons [transgender women] are attacked is because they do not possess that piece of anatomy", professor Cael Keegan said.[22]

The idea that millions of anti-Trump protesters represented a danger to trans people – instead of the hope of struggle that trans people would be empowered by – reflects the elitist thinking of queer theorists. Mass action is threatening because it involves individuals whose views on gender do not perfectly mirror their own. In the case of the Women's March and the movement for abortion rights, even the most obvious allies of trans people – progressive women and young people – are deemed to ultimately fail the test.

In contrast, trans activists like Elaine Rita Mendus articulate a much more serious and sensible approach to struggle. She "absolutely understands the use of the pussyhat".

> [President Donald Trump] has come out very strongly against reproductive rights and has targeted people with vaginas... Cisgender women especially are targeted and transgender men

---

22. Compton 2017.

are obviously caught in the shot as well... There are transgender people being murdered or living in the streets all over this country, constantly, and transgender women and cisgender women need to be together on that front... All people need to work together to try to deal with that rather than worrying about this language policing or making of safe spaces, quite frankly... We need to work on dealing with the problems at hand, not a stupid hat.[23]

For the purists in their insular groups, a "stupid hat" is as great a crime against trans people as the Trump presidency it was fighting, proof that ordinary people cannot be their allies. For fighters like Mendus, the Women's March showed the potential for trans people, women and other oppressed groups to fight together because Trump attacks them all.

Rejecting fragmentary and navel-gazing politics is crucial now that trans people are beginning to fight back in numbers. The development of protests explicitly about trans oppression has been a positive one. Trans Pride and Trans Day of Visibility marches are growing as trans oppression becomes a more defined battleground in its own right. The internet, growing visibility of trans issues, and the corresponding backlash have helped to forge a more connected, political trans community. The task is to struggle alongside all those fighting against oppression, to convince them that capitalism is the root cause and that it is as workers that people have the social power to overthrow it. Trans people are as capable of being won to this argument as any other, but the dead-end of identity politics – that prides itself on division, purity and self-fulfilling pessimism – must give way to the politics of solidarity and class struggle.

Because trans people face daily harassment and abuse from the public, and often painful rejection from family and friends, it is understandable that winning active support among broad layers of workers can seem unlikely. Forging solidarity between

---

23. Compton 2017.

oppressed groups is a dynamic process, not a mechanical marching forward of ideas. Socialists must consciously intervene and argue for principled positions even when these are unpopular.

The Stonewall riots, for example, had a profound effect on the consciousness of the oppressed. The rioters proved to the participants of other social movements that they, too, suffered from injustice, and that they, too, were ready to battle the state. The self-empowerment of the oppressed gives them the confidence to argue with others for their right to be free. They become determined to "take no shit from no one"; ordinary people can no longer ignore the issue and are compelled to pick a side. Stonewall pushed the left and the movements to take a more strident stand on the question of homosexual emancipation, something they might not have done previously. In August of 1970, Black Panther Party leader Huey P Newtown came out strongly in favour of the gay liberation movements, and pointed out that it was their own struggle that forced him to grapple with the issue.

> Remember, we have not established a revolutionary value system; we are only in the process of establishing it… We have not said much about the homosexual at all, but we must relate to the homosexual movement because it is a real thing. And I know through reading, and through my life experience and observations that homosexuals are not given freedom and liberty by anyone in the society. They might be the most oppressed people in the society.[24]

Struggles of the oppressed can win the support of workers by courageously showing the way forward. Whatever an individual worker's initial prejudices, the sight of ordinary people fighting back and facing police repression and media demonisation can resonate with their own experiences. The success of cross-solidarity groups like Lesbian and Gays Support the Miners, as depicted in the 2014 movie *Pride*, is apparent in the fact that the

---

24. Newton 1970.

National Union of Mineworkers was instrumental in changing the British Labour Party's policy on gay and lesbian rights, and still marches at the head of London's annual Pride parade.

The most powerful engine for transforming ideas is the struggle in the workplace, at the point of production. Strike action demands a united, democratic and determined collective of workers drawing a dividing line between themselves and the boss. At these times, prejudice and oppression can more clearly be seen as an obstacle to that necessary unity. Under the oppressive atmosphere of work under the boss, workers with right-wing ideas feel more comfortable running their mouth. On the picket line, with the boss and the police as direct enemies, that same worker may link arms with a trans workmate out of sheer necessity. This already begins to undermine the divisive foundation of their prejudice. Workers who already support trans rights or see the need for unity can raise their voice and convince others that prejudice has no place in the struggle. Right-wing workers lose their influence, their courage to attack others, and often even their right-wing ideas themselves. Left-wing workers gain influence, arm others with arguments that will help win the struggle, and help create a culture of solidarity.

The example of a strike in Argentina's biggest printing factory demonstrates this clearly. Years of organising – notably by Trotskyist workers – led to the workforce taking control of the factory in 2014, after management planned to sack 123 of the plant's 400 workers. One strike in the years preceding the takeover involved the defence of a trans woman workmate. Management refused to allow her to use the women's bathroom, and forced her to change with the men. The workers' assembly voted to support their workmate and demand her right to use the women's bathroom. In an article for Left Voice, Nathaniel Flakin explains how this was possible:

A Trotskyist party, the Party of Socialist Workers (PTS), had been working in Donnelley for many years. They built up an anti-bureaucratic, class struggle tendency in the workforce that won a majority on the workers' council. They defended the principles of class independence, workers' democracy and feminism. Thanks to years of discussions with Trotskyists, many Donnelley workers understood that to defend their interests, they needed to fight every kind of oppression.[25]

One strike does not guarantee that workers become champions of this or that oppressed group. It does, however, turn them into a collective more conscious of its united aims, more bitterly opposed to the boss, more determined to defend one another against victimisation and workplace bullying.

Marxism locates the source of gender oppression in class society, the material role that the nuclear family, sexism, homophobia and transphobia play in facilitating capitalist exploitation. The exploited working class has unique social power to bring capitalism to its knees. Their collective resistance in the workplace can cut off the flow of profits and form the basis of a democratic economy and society. But the divisions that capitalism sows among workers must be overcome through argument and through common struggle. The working class must become the champion of all oppressed groups to ensure a victorious revolutionary struggle against capitalism.

Conclusion

Transgender oppression is a hideous reality of capitalist society. The attacks from the right are unlikely to end, and the economic crisis will leave working-class trans people, already deprived of so much, worse off than ever before. Yet there are positive developments that should be pushed further, including the coming out of many more trans people, improvements in social attitudes, some legal reforms for trans rights, and street protests against transphobia.

---

25. Flakin 2019.

Miles' book comes at a critical time and provides a very informative and wide-ranging overview of trans politics, throwing light on the nature of gender identity and trans oppression. As the book addresses so many questions, there remains much to be explored theoretically on any one of them. Leslie Feinberg's *Transgender Warriors* is an excellent companion with its extensive historical research, but Miles' contribution to contemporary debates on the left about trans identity and political strategy makes it essential reading. Together these books offer the theory, history and politics to win a liberated world.

References

Callander D, J Wiggins, S Rosenberg, VJ Cornelisse, E Duck-Chong, M Holt, M Pony, E Vlahakis, J MacGibbon, T Cook 2019, "The 2018 Australian Trans and Gender Diverse Sexual Health Survey: Report of findings", The Kirby Institute, University of NSW, Sydney.

Carter, David 2004, *Stonewall: The riots that sparked the gay revolution*, St Martin's Press.

Ciobanu,Claudia 2020, "A third of Poland declared 'LGBT-free zone'", https://balkaninsight. com/2020/02/25/a-third-of-poland-declared-lgbt-free-zone.

Compton, Julie 2017, "Pink 'pussyhat' creator addresses criticism over name", NBC News, 8 February. https://www.nbcnews.com/feature/nbc-out/ pink-pussyhat-creator-addresses-criticism-over-name-n717886.

Engels, Frederick 1902 (1884), *The Origins of the Family, Private Property and the State*, Charles H Kerr & Co. https://balkaninsight. com/2020/02/25/a-third-of-poland-declared-lgbt-free-zone.

Feinberg, Leslie 1996, *Transgender Warriors: Making history from Joan of Arc to Dennis Rodman*, Beacon Press.

Flakin, Nathaniel 2019, "When workers went on strike to defend a trans colleague – and ended up occupying their factory", Left Voice, 22 June. https://www.leftvoice.org/when-workers-went-on-strike-to-defend-a-trans-colleague-and-ended-up-occupying-their-factory.

Hanrahan, Catherine 2019, "Are there more than two genders? Australia Talks survey reveals split in opinions", ABC News, 20 November. https://www.abc.net.au/news/2019-11-20/gender-diversity-splits-australians-in-australia-talks-survey/11714302.

Holcombe, April 2019, "'Religious Freedom' a euphemism for homophobic oppression", *Red Flag*, 21 July. https://redflag.org.au/node/6842.

James, Sandy E, Jody L Herman, Susan Rankin, Mara Keisling, Lisa Mottet, Ma'ayan Anaf 2015, "The Report of the 2015 U.S. Transgender Survey", National Center for Transgender Equality. https://transequality.org/sites/default/files/docs/usts/USTS-Full-Report-Dec17.pdf.

Miles, Laura 2020, *Transgender Resistance: Socialism and the Fight for trans liberation*, Bookmarks.

Milton, Josh 2020, "British newspaper apologises for 'dehumanising' cartoon portraying trans people as 'predatory'", Pink News, 23 February. https://www.pinknews.co.uk/2020/02/23/morning-star-trans-political-cartoon-labour-party-pledge.

Munro, Surya 2005, *Gender Politics: Citizenship, activism and sexual diversity*, Pluto Press.

Newton, Huey P 1970, "Huey Newton on gay, women's liberation", transcript of a speech on 15 August 1970, Workers World. https://www.workers.org/2012/us/huey_p_newton_0524.

Shipman, Tim 2020, "Boris Johnson scraps plan to make gender change easier", *The Sunday Times,* 14 June. https://www.thetimes.co.uk/article/boris-johnson-scraps-plan-to-make-gender-change-easier-zs6lqfls0.

Truss, Liz 2020, "Minister for Women and Equalities Liz Truss sets out priorities to Women and Equalities Select Committee", speech transcript, 22 April 2020. https://www.gov.uk/government/speeches/minister-for-women-and-equalities-liz-truss-sets-out-priorities-to-women-and-equalities-select-committee.

Walker, Shaun 2020, "Hungary prepares to end legal recognition of trans people", *The Guardian*, 26 April. https://www.theguardian.com/world/2020/apr/26/hungary-prepares-to-end-legal-recognition-of-trans-people.

Choosing between life and capital in Latin America[1]

Jeffery R Webber teaches in the Department of Politics at York University, Toronto. His latest book is *The Last Day of Oppression, and the First Day of the Same: The politics and economics of the new Latin American left.* He is presently at work on *Latin American Crucible: Politics and power in the new era,* under contract with Verso. He was interviewed for *Marxist Left Review* by **Róbert Nárai**.

> *Let's start at an epidemiological level. How has the virus impacted the region so far?*

In terms of the sheer number of cases and fatalities, all existing official numbers provided by states in the region are highly dubious. But you still have some discernible trends. In the future, the most reliable data – as elsewhere – will be the distinction between average death rates over the last several years and death rates during the pandemic period. Such death-rate analysis is particularly revealing both because these figures are more difficult for states to conceal or fudge, and because it captures deaths both from COVID-19 and those excess indirect deaths caused by people with other ailments who were not able to access necessary medical attention due to saturated capacity in the health system.

The full extent of this information will only be known fully some distance into the future, and perhaps never fully in the most under-resourced states. Nonetheless, there are already some initial studies focused on this kind of death rate comparison of select cities in the region, and the results are alarming;

---

1. This interview was conducted on 15 May 2020. In the meantime, figures for deaths and infections in Latin America have increased significantly.

the high numbers also stand in stark contrast to the lack of attention paid to the Latin America scenario by the dominant international media compared to the coverage of Europe and North America.

As of May 11, according to data provided by the Pan American Health Organization (PAHO), there were 1.74 million reported cases of COVID-19 in Latin America and the Caribbean, and in excess of 104,000 reported deaths from the virus. The rate of spread is also increasing decisively. Whereas it took three months for Latin America and the Caribbean to reach one million cases, it took fewer than three weeks to roughly double that number. Last week alone there were some 20,000 additional reported deaths in the region, which represented a 23 percent spike over the previous week's numbers.

As of today (May 15), we know that the incidence of the virus in Brazil is escalating the most rapidly of any country in Latin America and the Caribbean, alongside severe scenarios in Peru, Ecuador and Mexico. Brazil has the highest level of COVID-19 cases and deaths across all indicators in the region. There were 203,165 confirmed cases and the official tally of deaths by the virus in the country was 13,999, but this is surely a dramatic underestimate. The healthcare system in Rio de Janeiro, for example, is completely overrun, as it is in a number of major cities elsewhere in Latin America and the Caribbean. Big cities throughout the Amazon have been hit punishingly, and the Brazilian Amazon is no exception. A mortality study carried out by the *New York Times*, for example, showed that the Amazonian city of Manaus, which has a population of 2 million, recorded 2,800 deaths in April alone, which is about three times its historical average of deaths for that month.

Peru has the second highest number of confirmed cases in the region after Brazil at 80,604, with 2,267 deaths, followed by Mexico with 42,595 and 4,477 confirmed cases and deaths, respectively. Chile's official number of reported cases is also high, in excess of 37,000, with almost two-thirds in the capital, Santiago. Reported deaths are still below 400, but these are the official counts of the state – not comparative mortality rates based on the historical average, as in the Manaus example – and as we know from earlier official reporting in Europe and the United States, the real mortality figures lag well behind the day-to-day death notifications in the media, which are invariably revised substantially upwards at a later date. In terms of health infrastructure and the wider socio-economic backdrop of society, of course, it is of significance that Chile is one of the richer countries in the region, even though access to that infrastructure is intensely uneven. So even with high numbers, the death rate as a proportion of cases is likely to be lower.

Ecuador, by contrast, has been severely hit in terms of mortality rate (2,338 confirmed dead), even though the absolute number of reported cases is relatively lower than in Chile, at 30,500. A *Financial Times* investigation revealed that in the province of Guayas alone (the province contains the major coastal city and coronavirus hotspot of Guayaquil), there were 11,500 excess deaths, or 459 percent higher than historically average mortality rates in the province, between the outset of the pandemic in Ecuador at the close of February and April 28, the last day of data analysed. This is instantaneously revealing of a feature of the present conjuncture that we'll get into more – that is, this is not merely a natural crisis; rather, the uneven scale and depth of the impact has everything to do with the social conditions operative in specific locations. Thus, Ecuador is in no position relative to Chile to deal with what's happening at the infrastructural level of its health system.

Patterns elsewhere are indicative of exceptionality. For example, Argentina, which neighbours both Brazil and Chile, has a distinctively lower rate of transmission (7,134 confirmed cases), death rate (353), and so on. It also has witnessed a notably more extensive response from the state that helps to explain this discrepancy – early, state-enforced social isolation even when there were few cases. Already there is pressure from capital to open up the country's economy at whatever cost to lives. President Alberto Fernández – a figure who emerged from the more conservative wing of Peronism, but who was drawn somewhat to the centre-left given the fact that he owed his presidential candidacy entirely to his vice-presidential co-runner, former president Cristina Fernández de Kirchner – is taking a stance quite distinct from the far-right government of Jair Bolsonaro in Brazil and, in other ways, from the conservative government of Sebastián Piñera in Chile and the centre-right administration of Martín Vizcarra in Peru. This could have important political repercussions coming out of the first phase of this crisis.

At a first bird's eye glance, those are some of the places that are intensifying – Brazil, Peru, Mexico, Ecuador, Chile – with Argentina as a contrast study. If, and more likely when, the virus hits Central America and the Caribbean in a more concerted way the results are likely to be devastating. Countries such as Honduras, Haiti, Guatemala, and Nicaragua are very poorly positioned in terms of infrastructure to cope with a wide-scale unleashing of the virus, and this is even before we consider the interacting premise of an unsurpassed global depression. If it takes hold in these areas in a significant way the disaster could be monumental.

In Venezuela, where the official indications are that the case (455) and death-rates of COVID-19 are remarkably low (10), we don't yet have an accurate picture of how severe the problem is, but as in the Central American and Caribbean cases just mentioned, the health system is monumentally ill-equipped to handle any significant outbreak – problems of a dearth of basic medical supplies, ventilators, personal protective equipment, reliable electricity, and so on are self-evident, exacerbated by prolonged economic depression and US sanctions.

There is also the issue of the vulnerability of the over 5 million Venezuelan migrants who have left the country since

2015 – Venezuela is now in the highest position in the world in terms of outward migration, overtaking Syria recently. More than 1.8 million of the total number of Venezuelan migrants are presently in Colombia. They are now in desperate straits because they are not eligible for emergency resources from the Colombian state, and the viability of the sort of petty informal labour and commerce many of them were engaged in until recently has been all but eliminated.

So there's a real trauma there, and some are attempting to return home by foot, although whether what awaits them there is actually superior to their present circumstances is questionable. Even if it's true that the rate of infection is low so far in Venezuela, the infrastructural degradation of the social functions of the Venezuelan state after successive years of extremely intense socio-economic crisis, combined with the morally destitute sanctions imposed by United States, means that Venezuela could easily become one of the worst affected countries in the region if conditions change. In host countries further south, due to border closures and lack of transport, Venezuelan migrants facing similar straits as those in Colombia – in Peru, Chile, and elsewhere – are more or less stuck where they are for the time being.

I think we are in very early days, but that's part of the basic regional pattern visible so far.

> *So the pattern so far is uneven. Could you elaborate on the underlying dynamics that explain that unevenness? For example, the health of the public infrastructure across states, the condition of the working classes and oppressed, and so on?*

It is very clear that even prior to the onset of COVID-19 the social situation in much of Latin America and the Caribbean had deteriorated gravely since at least 2013, and many of the modest but important improvements in poverty rates and income inequality achieved during the era of progressive governments and capitalist dynamism driven by a global commodity boom (2003-2012) had already been significantly reversed.

The pandemic will exacerbate these conditions sharply. This week, the United Nations Economic Commission for Latin America and the Caribbean (ECLAC) published a projection of expected poverty increases in 2020, based on their conservative calculation of what constitutes poverty. The report suggests that there will be 28.7 million more poor people, and 15.9 million additional extremely poor people in the region by the end of this year. Added to the existing numbers of impoverished and extremely impoverished people, the total projected figure of poor people by the end of 2020 is 214.7 million, or 34.7 percent of the region's population, while there will be a total of 83.4 million extremely poor people should their conservative projections prove accurate.

Latin America has long been the most unequal region in the world, and it remained so even after the so-called Pink Tide experiments of left- and centre-left governance in the early part of this century. That inequality feeds directly into deeply stratified underlying health conditions and health access among the population.

Poor Latin Americans and Caribbeans are more vulnerable due to the higher prevalence in this layer of the population to existing conditions like lung or heart disease, diabetes, and general lack of access to sufficient medical attention. Likewise, class injustice is interlaced and intensified by the complex and specific oppressions of gender and sexuality, ethnicity and race, disability, homelessness, incarceration, and migration – all of these will mean disproportionate suffering by specific sectors of the population.

Speaking at a general regional level – and thus necessarily concealing a heterogeneous reality – health systems in Latin America and the Caribbean tend to lack both skilled medical professionals and medical supplies. There has long been an underinvestment in health by central governments, reaching an average aggregate regional level of only 2.2 percent of Gross Domestic Product (GDP). Most countries of the region have fragile and unintegrated health systems, which have not and will not be able to cope properly with COVID-19 as the crisis expands and endures. In most countries public healthcare is only directed toward low-income sectors of the population, and thus is underfunded and inadequate. Formal sector workers are often able to access the health system through social security services attached to their employment. The rich and powerful rely on private healthcare, whether in their home countries or abroad. Again, with variation, health systems in the region tend to be unequal in terms of access and quality.

The region's medical supplies and inputs are heavily dependent on global health supply chains that are breaking down logistically and politically at the moment, and most states in the region cannot compete with the bulk-buying power of imperial states in the world system, which are able to monopolise purchases of tests and personal protective equipment, among other supplies and equipment. Hospital beds and ventilators per capita are in most countries remotely distant from what is necessary even in normal times.

To make matters still worse, several health systems in the region were already coping – or better, failing to cope – with an outbreak of more than three million cases of Dengue virus in 2019 – over 2.2 million cases in Brazil.

A partial exception to these trends is the Cuban example. As is well known, one of the major enduring successes of the revolution is the island's healthcare system, which has an unusually high number of doctors per capita, and a history of well-coordinated preventative care arrangements. Early regulation on incoming flights from abroad, strict controls of mandatory physical isolation, extensive medical surveys and widespread check-ups on households by medical students, among other measures, have translated into weeks of declining new cases and a low death rate. The respective number of confirmed cases and deaths as of May 15 is 1,830 and 79. Continuing its history of international medical solidarity, Cuba has dispatched more than 2,000 doctors and healthcare workers to more than 20 countries, adding to the existing 37,000 Cuban medical personnel stationed in 67 countries around the globe. I say Cuba remains a partial exception despite these impressive details mainly because the internal economic contradictions in the country are severe, and the socio-economic fallout of declining remittances from the Cuban diaspora and a prolonged slump in tourism will likely have a serious impact on overarching conditions, even if the health system remains highly functional. The US sanctions regime persists, and could escalate in the lead-up to the American November elections.

> *So on the one hand, the pandemic is lighting up the vast class disparities that exist in terms of public health and livelihoods. On the other hand, the pandemic is entering a region that has been wracked by a series of pre-existing crises – economic, political, social and ecological – as well as one of the largest waves of popular rebellions we've seen for quite some time. How is the pandemic interacting with and exacerbating these pre-existing crises across the region?*

I think the most important element to highlight at the outset is that many of Latin America's major economies – Venezuela, Brazil, Argentina, in many respects Mexico as well – alongside many of its smaller economies, were already experiencing severe recessionary trends or low growth for the past several years. So there was a pre-existing economic crisis or recession in much of the region that was itself a kind of delayed reverberation of the 2008 crisis into Latin America.

That delayed reverberation was important in at least two respects. First, it was still mainly centre-left and left governments in office when the crisis started to really take hold in South America around 2012 and into 2013. And, second, to make a long story short, the centre-left and left governments which were in power shifted rightward by and large, implementing overt or disguised measures of austerity in response to the crisis, losing in the process significant swathes of their popular social bases while simultaneously failing in their bid to project "credibility" to capital. As a result they have been significantly weakened in political terms by that crisis, opening up opportunities for both extra-parliamentary and parliamentary forces of the right, including military expressions of the new right – depending on which country we are talking about. The right won elections in country after country, and where it couldn't win electorally it took power through a revival of hard coups (as in Honduras 2009), soft coups (as in Brazil 2016) or some mixture of the two (Bolivia 2019).

This was all pre-pandemic. So the pandemic is arriving in a situation in which you have three dynamics going on at once: newly formed right-wing governments in many countries; weakened and rightward-moving left governments where they remain; and, the main source of hope, new extra-parlia-mentary social movements – reaching semi-insurrectionary levels in places like Chile – especially in countries where the right is in power. This new protest wave, including the popular explosions in Ecuador, Colombia and Puerto Rico in 2019 (as part of an international uplift in radical protest that year), but also elsewhere in the region on a less visible scale, was rarely connected or well-integrated into any traditional left forma-tions, especially given the relative delegitimation of centre-left and left parties from their recent time in office in a number of cases. At the centre of the protest wave in many locales has been a resurgent popular feminism, with an intensity and depth perhaps without historical precedence in the region, and ecologically-based struggles.

These, then, were three of the prominent pre-pandemic political dynamics. It should be stressed that the new right governments in office were very far away from enjoying some sort of new hegemony, in the sense of replacing the old centre-left hegemony achieved at the height of the commodity boom. They were generally having difficulties governing, with very low rates of approval. In part, this is because they were unable to generate a kind of renewal of capitalist dynamism, a way out of the economic crisis – dependent as this has been in the region on the restoration of life in the world market. So as the viral pandemic arrives it is interacting with some of these basic political-economic scenarios.

Then you need to relate this to the basic crisis of capitalism on a global scale – insofar as the recent, robust rate of growth in Latin America between 2003 and 2011 was massively dependent on external dynamics – overwhelmingly, China's rapid industrialisation, high commodity prices, and so on. The latest projections of the International Monetary Fund suggest –3 percent global growth in 2020, which is a six percentage point contraction from the 2.9 percent growth rate of the global economy in 2019. The World Bank is predicting a fall of world trade of between 13 and 32 percent this year. According to the United Nations Conference on Global Trade and Development (UNCTAD), the value of global trade has already fallen by 3 percent in the first quarter of 2020, with an estimated quarter-on-quarter decline of 27 percent in the second quarter. Commodity prices, meanwhile, plunged by a record 20 percent in March, led by the collapse of oil prices.

These economic phenomena on a world scale will find particular transmission routes into Latin America – fall in export prices for both primary commodities and manufactured goods (the region's economy has become increasingly dependent on export earnings since the transition to neoliberalism in the 1980s, a subordinate incorporation into the international division of labour intensified rather than reversed under Pink Tide rule); declining terms of trade for the region; collapse of remittances from migrant labour; capital flight (both the withdrawal of foreign capital into safer assets as well as the capital flight of domestic Latin American capitalists as they, too, shift their fortunes even more than usual into foreign banks and off-shore tax-havens); breakdown of global value chains for those countries most heavily involved in manufacturing (Brazil and Mexico, especially); and a collapse in tourism (Caribbean small island states to be particularly brutalised by this factor, although its effects will be widely felt throughout Latin America and the Caribbean). ECLAC envisions an extraordinary contraction in 2020, with a −5.2 percent aggregate growth rate, which is well below projected rhythms in Africa, South Asia, or the Middle East.

This is a crisis of unprecedented scale and complexity, a truly global depression – the Eurozone, China, and the United States are all in turmoil. A global recession was already in motion prior to COVID-19, rooted among other things in problems of massive corporate, household and government debt, facilitated by quantitative easing, ie. cheap money, alongside low rates of profitability, little investment, escalating inequality as cheap money flowed into speculative financial investment schemes, and so on. The viral pandemic has made this underlying economic trajectory monstrously worse.

At the heart of all of this is the monumental question of debt. On the one hand, there is the issue of debt weighing down centres of global accumulation such as the United States and China (a product of their response to the 2008 crisis), which, quite apart from all the unknowns that persist with regard to COVID-19, calls into question the viability of any massive counter-cyclical intervention reanimating these economies and in turn providing an engine source for the world market, as China briefly managed to do following the 2008 meltdown. On the other hand, as Adam Hanieh has demonstrated so effectively, there is the problem of the extraordinary indebtedness of countries in much of the Global South – and not just the poorest ones – which is inhibiting their ability to meet the public spending challenges necessary for any effective response to COVID-19. Even before the latest world conjuncture, two years ago, in 2018, 46 countries devoted more government spending to servicing public debts than they did on their healthcare systems as a proportion of GDP.

In Latin America, the 1980s and 1990s witnessed a surge in the influence of the World Bank, IMF, and Inter-American Development Bank. As key institutional vectors of imperialism they made access to lines of credit conditional on neoliberal structural adjustment programs. During the height of the Pink Tide era and the associated commodity boom these institutions receded dramatically from the regional picture. As the global crisis of 2008 made its entry into South America by 2012-2013, however, these institutions followed in its wake.

Before the pandemic, both Argentina and Ecuador had already entered into agreements with the IMF and both were struggling to repay their debts. Ecuador and Venezuela were also massively indebted to China – today, China is the world's biggest public creditor to the Global South through its Belt and Road Initiative, and, along with all the other imperial debt collectors, it is now calling for repayment from the impoverished states of sub-Saharan Africa and Latin America to which it loaned hundreds of billions of dollars.

So-called emerging markets as a whole owe $171 trillion in debt to a multitude of creditors. Debt restructuring will have to occur, but as the *Financial Times* has pointed out, it is ever trickier to coordinate primary creditors to allow for a haircut on debt repayments given that, unlike in the 1980s and 1990s when creditors were mainly banks and governments, dominant creditors today are an assortment of bond funds, the managers of which are signalling that they are ready to settle into long-term international legal disputes with recalcitrant governments and put a sustained squeeze on even the most hard-hit countries to extract payments for their investors.

All of this means that, already in crisis, Latin American states are now in situations of extreme vulnerability, although the specific channels through which the global crisis is making its way into Latin America varies according to country and sub-region.

To make matters worse, alongside the economic crisis, there are the ongoing ecological contradictions of extractive capitalism. As Robert Wallace and others have pointed out, structural transformations in extractive sectors such as agro-industry worldwide – and associated patterns of planetary hyper-deforestation – are deeply associated with the origins of COVID-19 and potential future viral threats of a similar variety. It is no coincidence that within the dynamics of world capitalism, some of Latin America's most potent social struggles and conflicts between the reproduction of life and ecosystems, on one side, and the interests of capital, on the other, in recent years have been rooted in those sectors that express the particular regional manifestations of the rise of extractive capital globally – agro-industrial mono-cropping, oil and natural gas extraction and mining mineral extraction. Such battlegrounds are in today's altered world assuming novel dimensions, given what we know about the political-economic and ecological origins of COVID-19, and specifically its connection to agro-industrial food production, rural displacement, deforestation, and subsequent flow through global value chains, logistics processes, and so on.

So there's that crisis, the crisis of ecology. And then there's the crisis of social reproduction, with social reproduction understood in the broadest sense of the best new Marxist feminist analyses, as all activities extending through the realms of paid and unpaid gendered labour involved in the generational reproduction of the working class. This can involve everything from the unpaid toil of raising children and feeding and clothing family members, to the waged work of a teacher providing education, or a healthcare worker providing care to the sick.

In Latin America and the Caribbean women are particularly

affected by the aggravated pressure on health systems because they constitute 72.8 percent of the total number of employees in the sector region-wide. In addition to assuming the front-line crisis work in the health system as the pandemic spreads, women are disproportionately burdened with the excess social reproductive labour involved in quarantine, such as the caring and home-schooling of children. Paid domestic workers, accounting for 11.4 percent of women's jobs in the region, tend to be disproportionately migrants, indigenous or Afro-descendant women. They lack access to social security and increasing levels of unemployment as employer families readjust their home budgets in the face of the crisis. As is the case internationally, in Latin America and the Caribbean instances of domestic violence against women and children are intensifying in contexts of quarantine and collapse of household finances.

The social-reproductive elements of the Latin American crises were visible long before the pandemic, and they were raised to the foreground of political life in recent years through what is arguably the biggest wave of popular feminism in Latin American history. The last five years have seen massive movements in Argentina and Chile, and important feminist currents in Mexico, Brazil and elsewhere. The popular feminist movement in Chile, for example, was the most important articulating factor of the largest wave of rebellions in that country since the fights against Pinochet at the end of the 1980s. Latin American popular feminism today possesses an extraordinary vibrancy.

Unsurprisingly, alongside this uptick in praxis, there has been an accompanying theoretical effervescence on the Latin American left, pivoting on conceptualizing the dynamics of social reproduction, and the inherent conflicts between the reproduction of life and the reproduction of capital.

Of course, the insights of the ecological and feminist struggles, important as they were in recent years, are still more important in the present scenario facing the region, and indeed the rest of humanity. The fact that these movements were among the stronger popular forces of recent years is one of the positive factors that will play into the contending balance of forces between life and capital as we emerge from the first phase of the pandemic and disputes over the character of the "new normal" that will emerge to replace it. There are few moments in world history where the competition between the value of production for profit versus the reproduction of life has been so starkly posed.

So to recap a very complicated scenario: you have a viral crisis interacting with a crisis of capitalism at the global level and its specificity in Latin America; you have a crisis of ecology expressed in the intensification of extractive capitalism across all of these dimensions; and you have a crisis of social reproduction. All of this, of course, something we'll get into, is related to political crises of all sorts. Heuristically, I've spoken of many distinct crises, but these are actually better thought of as constitutive parts of a unitary crisis.

> *That seems like a good point to move onto the immediate political consequences so far. How have capitalist states been responding to this multidimensional crisis? Depending on who is in power and where, are there any early indicators so far as to how they are dealing with this crisis?*

Let's start with Brazil as it is the most important expression of the far-right in office responding to this crisis, and is also the biggest economy in the region and the most powerful Latin American country geopolitically speaking. Brazil is also a kind of exemplary condensation of the kind of crises that predated the pandemic and that have been interacting with the pandemic.

In Brazil – as in the wider international alt-right ideological milieu of post-truth irrationalism – you already had a formal attack by the Bolsonaro regime on the legitimacy of scientific evidence and the pursuit of scientific truths *per se*. We witnessed this with regard to the question of climate change denialism – the fires in the Amazon last year were, according to Bolsonaro, a conspiracy conjured up by NGOs, and, contradictorily, even if they did exist, it was the NGOs that set them alight in the first place – and myriad other mythologies and alt-right conspiracies of this sort, and even more bizarre ones. This was accompanied by legislative attacks on funding for healthcare infrastructure and scientific institutions alike. All of this meant that a kind of hyper-irrationalism, at the centre of all far-right positions historically, has meant that the most culturally authoritarian section of the Bolsonaro government – which is only about a third of the actual composition of the government, but a very important one, including the president himself – has seized upon the COVID-19 conjuncture and declared the virus a petty cold, a mere sniffle, nothing to see here, continue as usual.

Bolsonaro himself is widely believed to have tested positive for the virus, although he denies this, and continues to greet crowds of right-wing evangelical supporters with handshakes and smiles, interspersed with coughing fits. Bolsonaro's efforts from the executive to prevent people from physically distancing from one another, and the woefully inadequate economic measures the central government has taken in order to respond to the crisis, have meant persistent confrontation between the president and various state governments, including those of Rio de Janeiro and São Paulo, where governors attempted to institute some measures with the resources available to prevent an even greater catastrophe. Luiz Enrique Mandetta, Bolsonaro's minister of health, refused to go along with the president's absurdities and rooted himself in the scientific advice of epidemiologists. He was consequently dismissed from his position and replaced by yes-man Nelson Teich, a private healthcare capitalist with a degree in medicine and an MBA in business management. Bolsonaro's wilful disregard for human life in the context of COVID-19 is on a par with Trump's.

The historian Forrest Hylton has rightly labelled Bolsonaro "Brazil's Gravedigger-in-Chief".

Immediate schisms began to emerge from within the Brazilian regime as a result of Bolsonaro's cavalier disregard for the scale of what faced the country. To be sure, these schisms were already apparent in the Bolsonaro government in a more subterranean form prior to the pandemic, with the key fissures cutting through what I have called elsewhere a faction of cultural authoritarians pivoting around the figure of the president and his Rio-based familial dynasty, including his notorious sons; then a faction of militarists, pivoting around the vice-president, but also extending into all echelons of the state, from ministerial to lower technocratic and managerial positions in sub-ministries and public enterprises; and, finally, a faction of neoliberal technocrats, including the minister of the economy, Paulo Guedes, and, until very recently, the minister of justice, Sergio Moro. To repeat, these schisms were already present, with the government seemingly being held together over its first year by some sort of always fragile adhesive substance.

After several months of initial stasis in power, the Bolsonaro government managed to pass the thoroughgoing pension reforms masterminded by Guedes, the key Chicago-Boy finance minister. As a result, the markets began to come back on board with the government, after they had grown sceptical of Bolsonaro's capacities over the initial months of the new government.

Now, however, in the midst of the pandemic scenario, the justice minister, Moro, has resigned, and called into question Bolsonaro's legitimacy as president due to his interference with the federal police, who are investigating his sons for corruption and involvement in other crimes, crimes that extend all the way down to the militias involved in the assassination of Marielle Franco. The new intensity of this neoliberal technocratic-cultural authoritarian schism is very serious, and could eventually spell the end for Bolsonaro's presidency.

Although I don't think it's obvious that he will be ousted from office – people have announced his immediate demise every day since Moro resigned, a few weeks ago now. I don't think it's necessarily imminent, given that he retains 30 percent support of the population, which has always been about what his core base was, and it really depends massively on what action the military decides to take. The military faction of the regime has always had an enigmatic relationship with the president, not always free of tension, despite the fact that Bolsonaro himself is a former army captain. What is key in the Brazilian situation is that Bolsonaro's flagrant disregard for scientific evidence, and the dispute with his own minister of health and a series of state governors who tried to introduce some minimal measures to contain the spread of the virus, have jeopardised the lives of millions of Brazilians. I think the most important and disturbing thing about the crisis of Bolsonaro's rule at present is that the fissures are not a product of pressure from below, and that therefore will not obviously benefit social movements and the left. The main dispute in Brazil today, which might end up undermining the president's rule, is a schism between the centre-right and the far-right, neither of which have a particular allegiance to even the limited formalities of liberal democracy – which isn't to say that they are the same as one another. An eventual fall of Bolsonaro from office would not give an obvious momentum to the left, even if it would be happily greeted, unless popular movements can somehow play a bigger role than they have in instigating his demise.

In Bolivia, the dictatorship that was set in place following the coup last October, which removed Evo Morales from office, has used the arrival of the pandemic to postpone scheduled elections that were already going to be highly questionable. So a consolidation of power, of sorts, has at least temporarily unfolded in the country under this far-right regime. The spread of the virus in Bolivia has so far been minimal, however, so it's future destabilising effects remain unpredictable.

In Chile, there are political tendencies and counter-tendencies, the precise momentum of which remain difficult to discern with any precision. On the one hand, Piñera's regime has seemingly benefited in the short term, as the virus has provided cover for a suppression of the popular movements of recent months. His approval ratings have gone from a low of 9 percent to 25 percent, and the use of security forces in the streets to enforce mandatory physical distancing has been met with wide-scale approval – the same security forces that were so roundly discredited only weeks earlier.

On the other hand, the momentum of street politics and, in particular, the militant feminist wave is unlikely to simply disappear. Rather, it is set to play a decisive role in the battles over the new normal to come, once street politics is once again a reasonably safe pursuit. Karina Nohales, a militant involved in both the Committee for Workers and Unionists and the International Committee of the country's most important umbrella feminist collective, the Coordinadora Feminista 8M, explained recently that, despite being locked down, activists have managed to launch a Feminist Organization of workers. It is envisioned as a space in which women and militant workers come together from the perspective of their labour, whether it be formal, informal, paid or unpaid. Nohales describes the initiative as seeking to unite, in this way, wide layers of Chilean non-unionised workers with existing trade union militants in a space where all can participate and contribute, realising in this way the potential power of Chilean workers which until now has remained fragmented. The uniting strategic horizon is the Feminist General Strike – precisely what will be needed in coming months and years.

In Ecuador, you have a situation in which Lenín Moreno already entered into an agreement with the International Monetary Fund, which involved austerity measures designed to hollow out public infrastructure and the social functions of the state, including healthcare. Austerity measures were at the heart of a popular rebellion in October 2019, which witnessed the rearticulation of a popular indigenous movement at the forefront of class struggle. In the context of the pandemic, the rightward trajectory of the Moreno regime is being further concretised, as he moves to renegotiate debt with creditors and renew agreements with the IMF. As in Chile, it is difficult to imagine the momentum of the rebellions of October 2019 being completely eclipsed by the present interregnum.

In Argentina, where Alberto Fernandez sits at the head of a centre-left administration, the government is thus far enjoying a boost in popularity, despite a catastrophic economic crisis in which debt negotiations are ongoing and a major sovereign debt default is foreseeable in the near future. As I suggested, Fernandez took early, concerted action to enforce physical distancing measures, which won popular approval and also favourable treatment in much of the media. It helps to have Bolsonaro as the standard against which one is measured. The right-wing opposition has been discredited, and basically has subordinated itself to Fernandez's handling of the crisis. Mauricio Macri, leader of the preceding centre-right government, introduced a 23 percent cut to the health budget, further undermining the country's capacity to deal with the present crisis. Public health provision and the role of healthcare workers are being revalorised in the public consciousness in the midst of the crisis, laying the basis for future potential inroads against neoliberalism.

As Claudio Katz has explained, the pandemic managed to push the looming issue of debt repayment to the back burner, as public funding was immediately needed to service the viral crisis. Momentum has been behind a more confrontational stance with international creditors. At the same time, as elsewhere, Argentine social movements are crippled by their inability to assemble in the streets. There is a danger that the use of much-hated security forces to enforce mandatory physical distancing and isolation measures will be normalised post-pandemic, together with the extension of surveillance mechanisms. Illegitimate repressive measures taken by the security forces during the last couple of months have not been met with any reprisal from the Fernandez government. Alongside emergency cash-transfer measures that target informal workers and that seem to run against the logic of neoliberalism, Fernandez is at the same time making austerity moves, such as delinking unionised workers' future salary increases from inflation increases. As is the case elsewhere, one also has to include in this measure of the conjuncture the increasing pressures from capital in Argentina on the government to fully reopen the economy, whatever the cost to lives.

> *Could you say a bit more about what is taking place in Venezuela at the moment?*

Sure. There was another coup attempt against Nicolás Maduro. Until this latest fiasco, it would have been difficult to imagine a set of political events more farcical than that of Juan Guaidó's debacle in April 2019. In that case, likewise an effort to overthrow Maduro, Guaidó was only capable of mobilising a tiny faction of troops in the capital for a couple of hours, despite enjoying the full-throated support of the US and allied right-wing states all over Latin America. That earlier attempt revealed the limits of US imperial power in the region, given that it was obvious that they had played a decisive role in the coup plot. What the events of last April did not show was some kind of widespread popular backing of the Maduro administration or an indication of Maduro's success in the mind of the Venezuelan populace. Maduro's administration has been a disaster and has in my opinion no longer anything to do with the left. But obviously this has nothing to do with the question of opposition to imperialism as a matter of principle – it was a duty of all the international left to oppose the coup attempt by Juan Guaidó and the prospect of any potential US military involvement, or proxy involvement through Colombia.

The recent scenario involves some of these factors, but it is not obvious it enjoyed US backing, and whether or not that ultimately is shown to be the case, the whole endeavour was a complete and utter joke, hardly deserving of analysis. The usual instantaneous commentariat have compared it to the Bay of Pigs, but the events are not remotely comparable.

Effectively, Jordan Goudreau, a former US Green Beret, special forces veteran, who served tours of duty in Iraq and Afghanistan, and is now CEO of a Florida-based gun-for-hire mercenary enterprise called Silvercorp, coordinated the entire effort. The premise was to launch an attack on Venezuela by sea, seize an airport, kidnap Maduro, and fly him to the United States where he would face prosecution. Goudreau apparently ran training camps in anticipation of the assault on the Colombian Caribbean peninsula of La Guajira, adjacent to the Venezuelan border. The training camps were infiltrated from the start by Venezuelan government double agents, which accounts for the fact that, in the event, two boats were easily seized by Venezuelan troops, eight mercenaries were killed, and a couple of dozen Venezuelan accomplices were detained by the Venezuelan government, together with an American special forces operator from Texas named Luke Denman. It was over before it began.

> *Let's end with the question of popular movements. Apart from some very limited strikes among sections of workers, and some protests by medical professionals, there appear to be no discernible and sustained patterns of popular struggle, at least just yet. This is not to say that the basis isn't being laid for such struggles in the very near future. What do you think are the parameters of these struggles that are currently being laid by this crisis?*

I agree with your assessment that this precise moment is a weak one for popular movements, who are unable to engage in their usual above-ground assembly and repertoires of contention.

We can't know what's coming next, but we can speculate in a reasoned and relatively informed way, basing our analysis on the observable if contradictory tensions in the region's politics that are becoming visible.

In one direction, there is the potentially negative consequence of normalising a certain subservience to state authority in the wake of necessary cooperation around public health measures. The gravest dangers here are associated with the extension and normalisation of military and police power into everyday governance of public life in parts of the region, and the danger this poses to the revival of popular protest once the lockdown phase of the pandemic draws to a close. Likewise, in Latin America and the Caribbean, as elsewhere, there has been an extension of corporate surveillance facilitated by state measures responding to COVID-19. Capitalist states, while engaging temporarily in public health measures, are ultimately orientated toward restoring conditions for profitability, and insofar as an extension and consolidation of the role of the coercive apparatus of capitalist states is necessary for establishing post-pandemic conditions favourable to capital, states are likely to pursue this kind of normalisation if it is not resisted.

Another issue is the basic one that, for the moment, because social movements are demobilised and are capable only of virtual coordination through social media and the like, political momentum and initiative is very much in the hands of state managers and capitalist interests. This advantage in the immediate field of contention could position them well in determining the subsequent terrain to follow.

Critically, capitalist states are accruing significant debts, and the ensuing economic depression will demand sharper decisions from state managers as to who pays for the accumulated debts, and who is to benefit from the conditions of the new post-pandemic normal. The battle to come in Latin America and the Caribbean in the immediate above-ground, post-pandemic period will likely be structured in the first instance by capital-led austerity drives.

At the same time, working in the other direction is the ideological factor of this multidimensional crisis, making more visible than normal all of the interlaced threads of contra-diction, from ecology to social reproduction, as well as their connections to capitalism as a system. Critiques of the *system* of capitalism are likely to meet with a wider audience in the midst of this crisis. More visible to many is the basic irrationality of the pursuit of profit over life, the basic irrationality of ecolog-ical degradation attached to the system, the basic irrationality of attaching no value to socially reproductive work in normal times in terms of wages and conditions, and then celebrating it as "essential" in times of emergency; cheering healthcare workers on, calling them heroes, but not actually paying them decently, or providing them with effective equipment. There is no automatic process of politicisation attached to this, but in times of immense crisis people are more open to universal change of worldview than at other times.

So what is being valorised at this moment in popular consciousness in many Latin American and Caribbean countries in crisis is the notion of public health as a priority over profits, essential workers as necessarily having value attached to them, public services as a necessity, free access to the means of life, and so on. When the theatre of politics shifts from the present subterranean underworld of living rooms to above-ground workplaces, streets and communities, so will surface the tendencies and counter-tendencies I've cursorily noted above. The balance of forces aligned behind each side, drawing on reservoirs of strength extant in the pre-pandemic period but necessarily altered by the social, economic, and ideological conditions of the pandemic itself, will help to determine the content and form of the new normal.

That contestation, in the midst of an unprecedented global depression, will define the parameters of class struggle in the immediate future in the region. The outcome is not preordained, as it never is, but especially because crises are unusually contingent periods, in which various competing exit routes are opening and closing over the course of each battle.

This crisis shares some features with global crises of the past, even as it has other, unprecedented characteristics specific only to this moment. Insofar as we can learn from past crises, it is certainly the case that they don't automatically produce gains for the left. Such success will be contingent on strategies of intervention that mobilise and amplify the infrastructures of rebellion that exist where they do exist, flexibly respond to the genuinely novel reconfigurations of politics, economics and society coming out of the pandemic, and audaciously refuse to shrink for the scale of the change that is necessary simply to pull the emergency break and avoid disaster – after which and out of which a new world organised around our terms of life might be possible.

JACK CRAWFORD

Review: Resistance to the Accord

Jack Crawford is a PhD candidate in history at Adelaide University and a member of the NTEU.

Liz Ross, Stuff the Accord! Pay up! Workers' resistance to the ALP-ACTU Accord, *Interventions, Melbourne, 2020.*

HE PRICES AND Incomes Accord, known as the Accord, between the peak union body, the Australian Council of Trade Unions (ACTU), and the federal Labor government of Bob Hawke, was signed in 1983. In 2013, 30 years later, union and business leaders gathered at Macquarie University to celebrate its legacy. Standing among former ACTU royalty – Hawke, Bill Kelty, Simon Crean – then-president Ged Kearney addressed the crowd:

> The Accord was a highpoint of the political and industrial wings of the labour movement... Both realised they could not repeat the disunity that characterised the Whitlam years and could achieve more by working together even if that meant sacrifice and compromise.[1]

Funnily enough, there were no rank-and-file unionists in the room.

Indeed, workers have no reason to celebrate the Accord. Union membership and industrial muscle plunged during the Hawke-Keating years of federal Labor governments

1. Kearney 2013.

from 1983-1996 and afterwards. Today, striking is effectively outlawed. We owe to the Accord the plummeting of wages as a share of GDP, and the soaring of corporate profits.

Marxist historian Liz Ross' new book, *Stuff the Accord! Pay up!*, provides a left-wing answer to the self-congratulations of ACTU officials and Labor politicians. It arms readers with an essential socialist critique of the Accord. Uniquely, it focuses on workers' resistance in the Accord years, unearthing a hidden history of struggle from which union activists can draw lessons and inspiration.

Ross demonstrates how the Accord was the vehicle for the introduction of neoliberalism in Australia. High strike levels from the late 1960s had brought workers gains. Despite Labor Prime Minister Gough Whitlam's attempts to make workers pay for the world economic recession of 1974, Australian capitalism failed to deal a counter-blow to unionism that would sufficiently restore profit rates. The class struggles during the subsequent conservative government of Malcolm Fraser (1975-1983) produced a stalemate of sorts. It was not until Labor returned to power, wielding its authority to call for restraint among workers, that corporate Australia could sit comfortably.

Under Labor, unions sold away their right to strike and accepted wage restraint in return for the government's promises of "social wage and workplace benefits". As the years went on, and with union officials enmeshed in this framework, the Accord's proponents turned more explicitly towards "a focus on restraint, profits, productivity and competition" (p15). Over the course of the Accord, wages were cut in real terms. To their shame, the "left" unions controlled by the Labor Left or the Communist Party actively promoted this project of class collaboration. Union officials such as metalworkers' Laurie Carmichael effectively policed the working class, working to avoid strikes that might upset Accord arrangements. With unions having fitted their own straitjackets, Labor could oversee a dramatic redistribution of wealth from the bottom to the top.

Thatcher had destroyed union power with police batons. Hawke and Keating sought to do so with smiles and handshakes. But *Stuff the Accord!* will demolish any illusion that they could get away with this without facing serious resistance. Ross documents key disputes of the era, from Cockatoo Island's dockyard workers to Mudginberri's meatworkers to Queensland's electricity workers. Workers repeatedly fought to defend their rights, jobs, wages and dignity, bringing them into direct defiance of the Accord's strictures.

A definite highlight of the book is the Victorian nurses' strike of 1986, against the State Labor government. It is one of the longest strikes in Australian working-class women's history (surpassed only by the tailoresses' strike of 1882-3). The Accord did nothing to improve the situation of working-class women, despite its advocates' promises. No one knew this better than underpaid, overworked nurses. As one slogan put it, "Florence Nightingale is dead – so how come we're still getting her wages?" Rank-and-file militants drove the dispute, orienting to nurses' mass participation in pickets, marches and efforts to appeal for public support.

A militant strike against a Labor government threatened the Accord framework, and might set a dangerous example to other unions. The ACTU tried to undermine the nurses. Its president Simon Crean "personally attacked the union on several occasions, accusing them of 'demanding more than was justified' and advising them to go back to work" (p96). Even faced with this despicable lack of solidarity, the nurses emerged victorious, forcing the government to accept their wages and staffing demands.

The book is filled with such glimpses of workers' power. As late as 1995, Weipa workers proved how "old school" unionism – striking, picketing, campaigning for solidarity – could bring mining giant Rio Tinto to its knees.

However, the period is overwhelmingly a story of bitter defeats and frustrations. Ross stresses how the Accord destroyed bonds of working-class solidarity built in past struggles. Unions that stepped out of line to defend themselves from the employers' onslaught were usually isolated and crushed. Basic axioms of union solidarity – for instance, that sections of workers defending themselves helps defend the whole class – were dispensed with, replaced by the portrayal of strikers as "selfish" and "elite sections of the working class" (p18).

The Australian Federation of Air Pilots learnt this the hard way during their 1989 dispute. Hawke set out to crush the pilots' strike, warning, "It's a different game this time, boys. You go out and it's war". The prime minister declared a state of emergency, summoning the air force to scab on the strike and ensuring a crushing defeat for the pilots. The official union movement, by now loyal pupils of the Accord, "comfortably stood aside and let the pilots fall on their sword" (p180).

The deregistration of the Builders Labourers' Federation (BLF) – Australia's most radical union in living memory – was perhaps the Accord's most heinous chapter. The slogan "Dare to Struggle, Dare to Win" exemplified these workers' willingness to strike and win into the 1980s. From the perspective of the neoliberal Accord, the BLF had to be smashed. The gloves came off, with Hawke declaring to his cabinet, "We're going to smash those bastards". Struggling for their very right to a union, the builders labourers were mercilessly repressed. Union offices were raided, unionists arrested. The BLF had trounced the powers that be in the past. But this time, pro-Accord unions such as the Building Workers' Industrial Union were decisive in the destruction of the BLF.

Unionists ought to study these defeats. As Ross' book makes clear, deference to the Labor Party, to draconian anti-strike rules, and to our own conservative union leaders is fatal. Today's union officials are children of the Accord, by and large experts in spineless capitulation. At the time of writing, the leadership of the National Tertiary Education Union (NTEU) exemplifies this. With COVID-19 tearing apart the neoliberal model of higher education (due to a decline in high fee-paying international students) and the government refusing to provide necessary funding, university workers face the prospect of unprecedented attacks on their working and living standards. The NTEU's national executive immediately began collaborating with universities to alter enterprise agreements, offering to hand away hard won workers' conditions. This concessionary strategy, initiated in secret and then sold to members, is supposed to guarantee "a strong union role in managing the introduction of any cost-saving measures".[2] This epitomises the legacy of the Accord: don't *fight* "cost-saving measures", instead find a seat at the table when they are introduced. The rank-and-file revolt against the NTEU leadership's strategy offers a glimpse of the alternative: a recognition by workers that if we don't fight, we will lose for sure.

Rebuilding union power will require a daring defiance of calls for industrial passivity and self-sacrifice. It requires an ideological fight within the union movement. *Stuff the Accord!* is first and foremost a contribution to this fight, and should be read by anyone who wants to reverse the present crisis in trade unionism.

References

Kearney, Ged 2013, Address to "The Accord 30 Years On" symposium, Macquarie University, Sydney, 31 May 2013, https://www.actu.org.au/actu-media/speeches-and-opinion/ged-kearney-address-to-the-accord-30-years-on-symposium-31-may-2013.

Wood, Katie 2020, "University workers revolt against union concession plan", *Red Flag*, 25 April 2020, https://redflag.org.au/node/7149.

---

2. Wood 2020.

KATE DOHERTY

Review: The robbery of nature

Kate Doherty, a socialist activist since 2010, has been involved in campaigns for refugees and against the Adani coal mine.

John Bellamy Foster and Brett Clark, The Robbery of Nature: Capitalism and the ecological rift, *Monthly Review Press, 2020.*

NEW YEAR'S EVE 2019: 5,000 people on the beach at Mallacoota, Victoria, watch pitch-black skies turn a deep red as the bushfire approaches. They huddle, powerless against the fury of this climate change-fuelled nightmare. By March 2020, 33 people, one billion animals, 3,094 houses and over 17 million hectares of land had been destroyed in fires across Australia.[1]

June 2020: Coronavirus, a predictable product of industrial agriculture and deforestation pushing humans into the remaining reservoirs of wildlife, has killed over half a million people as we go to press, and the situation continues to escalate. Experts warn future pandemics are likely to increase in seriousness as environmental destruction worsens.

The scale and consequences of planetary destruction demand that we understand the ecological crisis and its roots. *The Robbery of Nature: Capitalism and the ecological rift* is a valuable contribution to this end. John Bellamy Foster and

1. Richards et al 2020.

Brett Clark argue for a fundamental transformation of society based on workers' control, and against the false solutions of green capitalism or hyper-technical state capitalism: "Ecological Marxism offers an opening up of humanity as a whole to creativity...to rebuild its world on ecological foundations in line with the earth itself" (p286). The serious application of Marx and Engels' historical materialism to wide-ranging but interlinked environmental issues makes this analytical volume a rewarding read.

Potatoes and cotton

> "As long as human beings exist, the history of nature and the history of human beings mutually condition each other." – Karl Marx (cited on p7)

The book's 11 chapters both defend and apply Marx and Engels' ecological thought. The authors respond to a range of historic and contemporary critiques and provide the reader with an opportunity to engage with Marxist understanding of nature from a number of angles.

Marx saw ecological destruction and that of humanity as intimately linked, as humans are both part of the natural world and rely on it for our survival. Capitalists expropriated the land, through brutal colonisation abroad and enclosures of peasant land in Britain. They ripped humanity from its natural connection with the land by creating private property from nature, and creating alienated human relations with the material world. Capitalism involves "the exploitation and squandering of the powers of the earth", just as it "squanders human beings...not only flesh and blood but nerves and brains as well" (cited on pp46-48). Whereas previously those who worked or lived from the earth were able to replenish it, capitalism introduced a "metabolic rift".[2] Separation of town and country ruptured the historic process of returning nutrients to the soil, and demands

2. The term, coined by Marx, is explained in detail in Kandelaars 2016.

on ecological systems increase as the needs of capitalism are imposed on nature.

The book's opening chapters focus on the two equally monstrous pivots of English modern industry – the import of potatoes from Ireland and slave-grown cotton.

Rack renting, the Irish land tenure system named after an instrument of torture, led to soil degradation and monoculture crops, making the country vulnerable to potato blight which struck from 1845-1849. While one million Irish died and a million more emigrated, the British continued the export of grain from Ireland: "Ireland was the site of an extreme metabolic rift, caught in the vice grip of economic and ecological imperialism, from which arose the necessity of 'ruin or revolution'" (pp72-77).

The triangular slave trade involved layers of robbery which enriched British capital. Humans were brutally stolen from Africa. Soil fertility, enriched by millennia of care by indigenous custodians, was also looted, exported as cotton fibre thousands of miles to England. The cotton industry rested on a "twofold slavery, the indirect slavery of the white man in England and the direct slavery of the black men on the other side of the Atlantic" (cited on p50).

Robbery is at the centre of capital accumulation.

An encompassing theory

Marx's ecology is inextricable from his social and economic analysis. The central section of the book demonstrates how environmental destruction is built into all facets of capitalism and how Marx and Engels' theories apply equally to modern issues. Certain chapters are unnecessarily academic, however the authors present Marx and Engels writing on a useful spectrum of topics. It is impossible in an article of this length to address each chapter, so just those on work, food, and wealth are addressed.

Revulsion towards work is not a constant feature of human society, but a product of the alienated organisation of labour under capitalism which makes work degrading, meaningless, destructive, and dehumanising (pp188-189). Certain sustainability theorists focus on expanding leisure and shunning work, arguing for a no-growth society. By contrast, the authors argue that while we must reject destructive work, "[t]he real potential for any future sustainable society rests...on its capacity to generate a new world of creative and collective work, controlled by the associated producers [workers]" (p174).

Marx's labour theory of value has given rise to the accusation that he perceived non-human nature as valueless. Yet it is capitalist logic that uses nature as a "free gift", as Marx observed. "Labour is not the source of all wealth. Nature is just as much the source of use values...as is labour, which is...the manifestation of a natural force, human labour power" (p163). For capital, labour in extracting and processing makes natural resources marketable.

It is no solution to put a dollar value on natural resources, as some environmentalists recommend. A truly perverse element of capitalism is that it feeds on scarcity, thus planetary destruction can open up new markets, monetising products which were once freely available in abundance. Gerard Mestrallet, CEO of global water corporation Suez, stated: "Water is an efficient product. It is a product which would normally be free, and our job is to sell it. But it is a product which is absolutely necessary for life" (p170).

"Food...is only of passing interest to Marx", asserted the 1992 book *The Sociology of Food* (p104). In fact, Marx was already grappling with the problems surrounding food in the 1850s. Chapter 4 charts Marx and Engels' study of the production, distribution and consumption of food. It encompasses agricultural development under different modes of production, soil chemistry, industrial agriculture, livestock conditions, food adulteration, climate, food production technology and much more. Their interest in food makes sense: a materialist conception of history is centred on humans as beings who must, before all else, produce the essentials – food, water, shelter etc. Capitalism makes a commodity of this essential good.

For revolution

In the final two chapters the authors outline the extent of the planetary crisis we face, and make a compelling case for the revolutionary potential of humanity to heal the rift with nature created under capitalism. "As bad as the climate crisis is...it is only a part of the larger global ecological crisis" along with ocean acidification, ozone layer destruction, biodiversity loss, freshwater shortages, pollution and others. The root cause of the ecological crisis lies in our socioeconomic system of capital accumulation (p244).

There are many who argue for substantial, but not revolutionary, changes to capitalism to combat ecological destruction.

Those who argued the coronavirus crisis was an opportunity for better climate outcomes are anti-human, but they're also plain wrong. Common sense suggests financial crises would cause a sharp drop in carbon emissions. But data from 150 countries between 1960 and 2008 has comprehensively demonstrated that emissions don't decline in the same proportion during downturns as they increase during growth.[3] The system is not going to self-limit. The drive to accumulate continues, even in light of an unprecedented health and financial crisis caused in part by environmental destruction.

The most polemical section of the book is dedicated to a critique of the current which aligns socialism with ecomodernism. The authors choose the *Jacobin* special issue *Earth, Wind and Fire* as their focus, which includes pieces arguing for nuclear power as the alternative to fossil fuels, terraforming (reshaping the earth), geoengineering (such as cloud brightening), mass carbon capture and storage as technical solutions.

The *Jacobin* writers critique the environmental movement

---

3. Richard York, "Asymmetric Effects of Economic Decline on CO2 Emissions", cited in Bellamy Foster and Clark 2020, pp242-243.

for "a politics of fearmongering and austerity" and urge the left to abandon the "aversion to ambitious technologies" and to love our monsters. "Green capitalists are the ones shaping the future", so socialists should look to state management of technology, the market and urban development, together with progressive redistribution of resources.[4] Their fundamental argument is that technological solutions are more realistic than, or preferable to, social revolution and workers' power.

The authors rightly point out that the domination of nature does not represent a scientifically feasible, or desirable, solution to environmental devastation. There are much better and faster ways to address the climate crisis than unproven and resource-intensive technology like carbon capture and storage, which would almost certainly widen other ecological rifts (such as deforestation and biodiversity loss). The current system is "built on waste. The [majority] of production is squandered...in such forms as military spending, marketing expenditures, and the inefficiencies, including planned obsolescence, built into every product" (p284). Thus drastic cuts in carbon emissions, pollution and wasted human labour are immediately possible through a revolution in social relations.

While their critique of the ecomodernists strikes true, the authors are on more shaky ground when they present their own solution to the crisis. They see the main impetus of environmental revolt in the "environmental proletariat", which they hope may arise from La Via Campesina, a millions-strong international peasant movement (p259). While agricultural workers and small landowners, particularly in the developing world, are materially driven to resist environmental destruction and are an important ally of any serious climate movement, a successful social revolution must centre on the industrial working class at the heart of capitalist production, who have the most power to bring the system to a halt.

---

4. Connor Kilpatrick, Angela Nagle and Daniel Aldana Cohen, cited in Bellamy Foster and Clark 2020, pp274-281.

The authors conclude: "To overcome centuries of alienation of nature and human labour, including the treatment of the global environment and most people – divided by class, gender, race and ethnicity – as mere objects of conquest, expropriation and exploitation, will require nothing less than a long ecological revolution...occurring over centuries" (p287). The history of revolutions indicates a socialist society focused on improving human life could make great strides towards these goals in the first months and years, though not without enormous difficulties. Though the authors do not suggest it themselves, their conception of revolution does not preclude reformist interpretations. This is a missed opportunity: the seriousness with which their works are read in the broad environmental movement means they are uniquely placed to make revolutionary arguments to wider audiences.

Overall, the urgency of the environmental crisis demands we recommit to, and deepen our understanding of, revolutionary politics and the connection between climate crisis and capitalism as a system. *The Robbery of Nature* is an excellent tool to help us do just that.

References

Kandelaars, Michael 2016, "Marxism and the natural world", *Marxist Left Review*, 11, Summer. https://marxistleftreview.org/articles/marxism-and-the-natural-world/.

Richards, Lisa, Nigel Brew, Lizzie Smith 2020, "2019–20 Australian bushfires – frequently asked questions: a quick guide", Department of Parliamentary Services, March https://www.aph.gov.au/About_Parliament/Parliamentary_Departments/Parliamentary_Library/pubs/rp/rp1920/Quick_Guides/AustralianBushfires.

SAM PIETSCH

Review: Occupation and resistance in West Papua

Sam Pietsch is the author of a PhD about Australia's military intervention in East Timor in 1999. He has been active in socialist politics for nearly two decades and is a militant in the Community and Public Sector Union in Canberra.

John Martinkus, The Road: Uprising in West Papua, *Black Inc., 2020.*

THE WEST PAPUAN independence struggle gained rare exposure in the mainstream Australian media in August 2019, when protests and riots shook the provincial capital Jayapura and a number of other towns across the occupied territory. The unrest was triggered when racist vigilantes attacked West Papuan students living in the Javanese city of Surabaya and Indonesian police intervened to arrest, not the perpetrators, but 43 of the Papuan students themselves. Video of the incident, including racist taunts hurled at the Papuans, circulated widely. As Martinkus writes, protests against Indonesian rule are nothing new, but in 2019:

> The scale of the protest and the determination of the protesters not to back down in the face of the usual security services response were unprecedented. Thousands took to the streets. They were chanting calls for independence, waving the Morning Star flag [the symbol of independence], condemning the institutional racism in Indonesian society that had labelled their students in Surabaya monkeys. (Chapter 7, paragraph 5)

Government buildings were torched in multiple towns, while

in Sorong 250 prisoners escaped from jail and the airport was briefly occupied by protesters. Dozens of people were killed in the riots and ensuing crackdown by the Indonesian police and military. Trials for treason of some of the activists arrested are ongoing at the time of writing.

For those wanting to learn more about the struggle in West Papua, Martinkus provides a short and readable account of the independence movement and the history of Indonesia's occupation. The book's style and content reflects Martinkus' work as a journalist. This is mostly a positive. Martinkus has long embodied the best journalistic traditions and has previously written books covering the conflicts in East Timor, Aceh, Iraq and Afghanistan. In *The Road*, he once again pokes his nose into places the powers that be would rather remain obscured; bringing to light the oppression and violence inherent in Indonesia's occupation; recording the resistance and courage of the West Papuans who fight back. There is no false "objectivity" here.

It's the sort of journalism which all too rarely makes an impact in Australia. Partly this is due to the Indonesian government effectively banning foreign journalists entering West Papua. Martinkus himself has not been able to enter the territory since 2003.[1] Those attempting to report illegally face arrest and imprisonment, and Martinkus strongly suspects filmmaker Mark Worth was assassinated by Indonesian security forces for documenting the independence struggle. The fate of the Balibo Five, reporters murdered by the Indonesian military to cover up the invasion of East Timor in 1975, still serves as a warning to foreign journalists.

But the Australian media is to blame as well. Martinkus caustically recounts when he was reporting on East Timor that an Australian editor asked him dismissively "So what are your plucky brown fellows up to today?" Martinkus learnt that a

---

1. A more detailed account of his own time reporting from West Papua has previously been published in Martinkus 2002.

body count of at least 10 was required before a story would be run; the daily violence and intimidation faced by those under occupation in places like West Papua is simply not considered newsworthy.

But *The Road* offers more than a collection of headlines. Martinkus usefully summarises the history of the conflict. When Indonesia won its independence from the Netherlands in 1949, West Papua remained under Dutch control. Indonesian nationalists campaigned to assume control of the territory in order, as they saw it, to complete the national liberation struggle. This included military incursions from the early 1960s. Seeking a way out, the Netherlands made preparations for West Papua to become an independent country. However, attempting to gain a Cold War ally, the United States backed Indonesia's territorial claims. Under the guise of a United Nations agreement, Indonesia assumed full administrative control from 1963.

Incorporation was given a fig leaf of legitimation by the 1969 "Act of Free Choice". For the benefit of United Nations observers, the Indonesian military selected just over 1,000 Papuans who publicly and unanimously voted to become part of Indonesia. The whole episode was an obvious sham, and West Papuans continue to demand a genuine act of self-determination.

Australia was one of the few countries which opposed Indonesia incorporating West Papua. Martinkus implies that this arose from principled support for decolonisation and recognition that West Papuans' interests would be best served by uniting with fellow Melanesians in Papua New Guinea. In reality, Australia had long supported European colonial powers controlling the Indonesian archipelago as a bulwark against rival powers such as China and Japan. Maintaining dominance over Australia's own colony in Papua New Guinea was considered vital. It was feared that if Indonesia, a rising Asian power in which the Communist Party was gaining strength, gained control of West Papua, Australia's own position would be threatened.[2]

These fears were eased in 1965, when the right-wing dictator Suharto came to power in a bloody coup, killing perhaps a million Indonesians and destroying the Communist Party, welcomed if not materially supported by the US and Australia. The Australian government for decades now has strongly opposed any suggestion West Papua should become independent, fearing the destabilising effect this would have on the entire island of New Guinea, which continues to be seen as vital to Australia's security interests.

But although the Netherlands was defeated, West Papuans themselves soon began resisting Indonesian control, including military action by guerrilla forces operating under the banner of the Organisasi Papua Merdeka (OPM, Free Papua Movement).[3] This prompted an intense military crackdown in the mid to late 1970s. The true death toll among West Papuans will probably never be known, but Martinkus cites estimates ranging from 100,000 up to half a million, most of them civilians prey to disease and starvation when they were displaced from their homelands.

Although at lower levels of intensity, the violence has never stopped. Even peaceful acts of opposition to Indonesian rule, such as raising the Morning Star flag, can result in arrest, imprisonment, torture or death at the hands of the security forces.

Fuelling the conflict is a struggle over who controls West Papua's land and abundant natural resources, symbolised by the construction of the Trans-Papua Highway, "the Road" of the book's title:

> For the Indonesians it was a symbol of success and development, something to be celebrated. For the Papuans it was like a spear

---

2. For details see Pietsch 2015, pp132-133.
3. Osborne 1985 provides details of the early years of the independence movement.

through the heart, killing their traditional life and claims on the land. (Chapter 3, paragraph 30)

Stretching from Sorong in the north-west peninsula to Merauke near the border with Papua New Guinea, the road facilitates access for Indonesian security forces and opens up the vast, mountainous interior of the territory to industries such as logging, palm oil plantations and mining. For West Papuans, it means dispossession, environmental destruction and poverty.

Such is the legacy of the giant Grasberg mine, located in the heart of West Papua's central highlands. Now co-owned by the Indonesian government and United States company Freeport-McMoRan, Grasberg is the largest gold and second-largest copper mine in the world, generating turnover of up to $2 billion a year. But little wealth reaches the local population, who have been stripped of their traditional lands and who must contend with devastating pollution produced by the mine. Indonesian security forces are paid protection money to defend the mine from protesting locals or pro-independence guerrillas.

It is a pattern repeated across West Papua. So although out of 34 Indonesian provinces West Papua and Papua are ranked sixth and eleventh in terms of wealth generated per capita, they are the two lowest ranked in terms of the Human Development Index.[4]

The economic situation is compounded by an issue barely touched on by Martinkus: the very substantial migration into West Papua from other regions of Indonesia, sponsored by the central government. The 2010 census already recorded around one-third of the population as being from non-Papuan ethnic groups, with migrants and their families strongly concentrated in major towns and more developed lowland areas.[5] The

4. Statistics Indonesia 2020, tables 4.6.7 and 15.2.5. Administratively, West Papua is divided into two provinces. The Human Development Index is a composite measure based on health, education and consumption levels of the population.

5. Elmslie 2017.

growing number of settlers may soon constitute the majority of the population.

So West Papuans are caught in the classic double bind of the colonised. Forbidden their independence, they are also denied the full rights which should accompany their formal status as Indonesian citizens and are dispossessed in their own land.

Little wonder, then, that resistance springs up again and again, despite years of oppression. Martinkus charts the latest resurgence back to a round of pro-independence demonstrations held in 2016. Mass arrests and intimidation of activists followed. Yet by early 2019, exiled independence leader Benny Wenda was able to present a petition calling on the United Nations to relist West Papua on the committee for decolonisation and demanding a genuine act of self-determination. A claimed 1.8 million signatures were collected clandestinely and smuggled out of the territory.

Supporting such efforts and heavily involved in the protests and riots of late 2019 is a new generation of Papuan youth and student activists:

> The students are part of a wave of empowerment of younger Papuans, who know their rights and are ready to stand up for and die for them, just as their fathers and mothers have before them. (Chapter 7, paragraph 38)

Against this background, the cover of *The Road* states "The war is not ending, it is beginning". But what are the prospects for the movement? Here, Martinkus' fairly impressionistic account leaves unanswered a range of questions. For example, he documents a revitalised military resistance, with better armed and organised guerrillas launching more effective attacks on Indonesian forces. But ultimately how effective is military action, and what is the relationship between the armed and civilian wings of the movement? There is likewise no detail on issues such as debates within the movement over strategy, organisational questions, or the role played by exiled activists as compared to those still in West Papua.

Martinkus frequently notes parallels with the East Timorese independence struggle, which was victorious in the context of a mass movement for democracy which forced Suharto from power. He highlights support for West Papuan self-determination from Indonesians such as human rights lawyer Veronica Koman and left-wing activist Surya Anta.

But such figures are isolated examples who face heavy repression from the Indonesian state, in the context of increasing attacks on democratic rights and freedoms within Indonesia itself. This trend is epitomised by the 2019 appointment as defence minister of Prabowo Subianto, a former general dishonourably discharged in 1998 for his role in kidnapping pro-democracy activists. Prabowo's Great Indonesia Movement Party participates in a grand coalition government led by President Joko Widodo, who many had hoped would be a bulwark for democracy. In this context, what sort of politics could provide a way forward for democracy activists in both Indonesia and West Papua? A more analytical work would have begun to address such questions, without necessarily providing definitive answers.

Instead, Martinkus gives us a moving if somewhat schematic account of the West Papuan struggle, which continues against all the odds, and deserves to be better known and supported in the outside world. He sombrely concludes:

> They can kill, jail and displace this generation, but there will be another one and another one. I hope I do not have to write this book again in twenty years, because if the Indonesians and the Australians and the UN continue their current policies in Papua, there will never be peace. (Chapter 9, paragraph 10)

References

Elmslie, Jim 2017, "The great divide: West Papuan demographics revisited", *The Asia-Pacific Journal*, 15, 2, 1, January 15. https://apjjf.org/2017/02/ Elmslie.html.

Martinkus, John 2002, "Paradise betrayed: West Papua's struggle for independence", *Quarterly Essay*, 7, September.

Osborne, Robin 1985, *Indonesia's Secret War: The guerrilla struggle in Irian Jaya*, Allen & Unwin.

Pietsch, Sam 2015, "Indonesian independence and Australian imperialism", *Marxist Left Review*, 10, Winter. https://marxistleftreview.org/articles/ indonesian-independence-and-australian-imperialism/.

Statistics Indonesia 2020, *Statistical Yearbook of Indonesia*, catalog 1101001.